THE WAYS
WE ARE TOGETHER

THE WAYS
WE ARE TOGETHER

Reflections on
Marriage, Family and Sexuality

by John Garvey

THE THOMAS MORE PRESS
Chicago, Illinois

Some of the essays in this book appeared, in different form, in *Commonweal, Doctrine and Life, Notre Dame Magazine,* and *U.S. Catholic.* They are reprinted here with permission of the original publishers, to whom I owe thanks. Thanks too to Peggy Rosenthal for a good quote.

ISBN 0-88347-153-1

CONTENTS

PREFACE

THE chapters of this book circle around a center which is so simple that we forget it: we conscious beings are incarnate. We inhabit particular flesh. We have gender, are male, female, heterosexual, homosexual, married, single, celibate; and all of us come from families—which is to say, we are the result of our parents' lovemaking.

Being human we try to put our experience of these things into words. We draw conclusions from our experiences, make rules, try to pass on good advice to our children. And in the depths of our heart we are confused about this whole matter of being incarnate, mortal, full of desire and the need to love and be loved. There are times—some of them important ones—when neither the secular culture nor the religious institutions which could offer an alternative vision seem to be much help to us in our attempt to be clear about these things.

This book certainly won't offer all the answers, and it may not offer any answers at all. But I hope at least to help this much: I hope that a restatement of some problems will help to clarify them—sometimes by making them as confusing as they really are. A look at history might make some confusing things not necessarily less confusing (since confusions about some aspects of marriage and sexuality have reigned since the start of Christianity) but less threatening. And finally I hope to evoke a sense of how odd it is that we are incarnate in this way. To see our oddness and limitation can refresh our perception and understanding, and if I do no more than bring that sense to the surface it will have been enough.

PART ONE

Marriage: Some of Its Complications and Delights

MARRIAGE: *AN INTRODUCTION TO SOME PROBLEMS*

NOBODY knows much about it. Married people have complained that celibate priests often speak too easily about marriage, as if they knew more about it than their married audiences. There is a point to the complaint: only someone who has experienced something has final authority about his own experience. He will need more than experience; but he will need at least that, if he is to be taken seriously as an authority. You wouldn't call a man a prophet if he had spoken to someone who spoke to God; and you can't call anyone who doesn't have an intimate knowledge of marriage a true authority. (This intimate knowledge is distinct from an intimate knowledge of married people, a valuable perspective which a priest may very well have. At some levels it is not the most important one.)

The trouble with this is that the married person who has an intimate knowledge of many other married people, and who can understand their experience by comparison with his or her own experience in a way which is not available to the celibate, is also married to someone who is the only sort of person he or she is. At its most intimate level marriage can be looked at only from the point of view of a person who has to live in that all-important, and limited, situation.

So we have a major problem at the outset: celibates don't know some things which matter deeply to married people, things which sometimes require a sensitive guidance of the sort only another married person might be able to offer; but at the same time, married people themselves are limited in their ability to offer help, because marriage is not at all an easy thing to generalize about, primarily because you are married to one sort of person (the only one of its kind on the planet), and your neighbor is married to another equally strange, unique human being.

Of the sacraments which Roman Catholicism and Orthodoxy have made "official" (and there will be more about sacraments shortly) marriage is the only one which we share with the rest of the human race. There are people who would argue that the sacramental aspect of marriage depends exclusively upon the Christian commitment of the people involved. This makes sense: Christianity reveals a depth to our ordinary experience which we would not see without its revelation; we would walk by it like sleepwalkers. But what it reveals is a human depth, a depth which all human beings share, and it is especially important to stress this in a religion which tells us that the Word—the meaning of everything which exists—became flesh. If sacraments are seen not only as rituals but as occasions for transformation, marriage's effect is in some ways more demonstrable than that of any other sacrament, and it is an effect (or a number of them) which happens as a result of participation in an evolving situation—a rite which doesn't end with ceremony.

Marriage is unlike other sacraments in presenting a reality which is in important ways available to people who are not Christian. That may seem a condescending way to put it, because of course non-Christians marry and of course what they learn from marriage matters deeply and transforms them as they learn. But it must be said this way because marriage is the only sacrament of which this is true, and there is no clear evidence that what is learned over the years in a non-Christian marriage is in any degree less transforming than whatever it is Christians learn. This is an important lesson in what incarnation means: there is something spiritually significant in marriage which is present whatever our intentions are, or whatever our religious orientation (or lack of it) is. A specific religious intention might help to make us attentive to what can come of being married; it might be a way of getting our attention. But what happens there can happen without it, in which case the religious intention is (like a coal-miner's lamp) an illumination of something which is already there. Marriage has been from the earliest times an important Christian metaphor—Paul compares the relationship of married people to the relationship Jesus has to his followers—but it is also a relationship which people who have no religious commitment can understand more than any other, one which has a religious profundity and a hopeful implication for people who do not attach themselves to symbols or sacraments in any other area of their lives.

If there is anything which cements us into the human race it is the decision to get married and have children. We may find ourselves at some moments wanting to find something which will dissolve that cement, but the decision to marry is, for most of us, not only a decision which we will come to regard as a serious and irrevocable one—it really is the one which forms us more than any other, and makes us, as we learn from it, and are changed by it, what we will be for eternity.

The commitment to marry has a depth which almost every other commitment lacks, because the stakes are so much higher. The closest thing to it is deep friendship, which also obligates us but in different ways. Even though it is not called a sacrament in every Christian church marriage is almost always treated as one—that is, as a profoundly important decision with sacred implications, one which involves the recognition that God's help is necessary if the marriage is to work at all. For people who are not religious it is (as movie director Robert Altman, who looked at marriages in his movie *Wedding*, pointed out in an interview) the last sacrament we have as a culture. People gather for this ritual as they do for no other. They celebrate something in common, and their hopes are gathered for awhile: they wish the couple well, and during the ceremony the married people present think a little more deeply than they usually do about their own marriages.

Given the respect we all seem to have for marriage, it might seem strange that marriage is so threatened today. The divorce rate is extremely high—higher than fifty per cent in some younger age groups—and this fact has profound cultural implications. The children of divorced parents are hurt by the experience, though in some cases the pain suffered by a child whose parents stay together may be much greater than the pain caused by divorce. Still the attitudes of children towards marriage are formed by the divorces of their parents or the parents of their contemporaries.

No one really likes this state of affairs. Most people who marry do so with every intention of seeing the marriage remain intact forever. People who make second and even third marriages usually do so with the sincere hope that *this* time it will work out.

What has brought us to this? What do people expect of marriage in our society which makes divorce happen so often? It is clear that our expectations have something to do with the problem. What should our expectations be?

First of all, it should be understood that the divorce rate isn't simply the product of moral decay. People live longer, and women are not nearly so likely to die during childbirth as they were fifty or one hundred years ago. The fact is that if a couple marry in their twenties they are quite likely to spend fifty years or more with each other, barring a divorce. They are likely to have fewer children during the wife's child-bearing years; much of their attention will necessarily go to the marriage itself, because most of the marriage will be lived through after the children have left home. And expectations about what marriage ought to be are higher than they were in the past. It isn't enough for a husband to be a good provider and the wife an adequate cook and housekeeper. That was never what marriage should have been, of course, but people were more likely to stay together for such reasons, and for the sake of the children, a generation ago. If marriage wasn't constantly unpleasant it was considered all right, something one could live with. And there were always enough dreadful marriages around to make one's own seem acceptable.

If the expectations people bring to marriage today are often unrealistic, this should not lead us to assume that the older expectations were necessarily better. I know of a family whose mother sent the children to a neighbor's house when the father came home drunk, knowing that she was about to be beaten. The children knew it, too, but left obediently when their mother asked them to, knowing what she faced. Today she would probably leave, saving herself and exposing the children to far less hurt than they experienced living through such terror. This was an extreme case, but it isn't all that uncommon, and in societies where a high premium is put on remaining married, no matter what, marriages probably do not break up as often as they should (a contrast to ours, where marriages which probably could be saved are often abandoned). In Ireland I met a woman whose mental health—what there is left of it—is maintained through a steady infusion of anti-depressants. She has two ungovernable children and a husband who drinks up the family money and is cruel to her. His threat is that unless she keeps him supplied with her own family's money he will leave her. In her small village a separation is unthinkable; so a marriage which simply should not continue is allowed to wound her and her children. The most she has to look forward to is widowhood. The only bright spot in all of this is that her husband's drinking habits are such that widowhood may not be far off.

Apart from these obviously destructive, blighted marriages there are other models of emptiness which are terrifying to young people considering marriage. I can remember seeing parents of my friends sitting together without speaking—usually in front of the television set—and whenever they did speak their words were not particularly affectionate. There is a silence between people who love one another which is full of peace; there is another kind which is so cold that it reminds you of an iciness worse than hellfire. A middle-aged woman I knew when I was in my late teens and wondering whether I wanted to be married, ever, told me that she didn't love or particularly like her husband, but stayed with him because neither of them had anywhere else to go.

"What do you *do*?" I asked her. What I meant was, what do you do when you both come home from work and find yourself together in the same house.

"We watch television until we're tired," she said.

That emptiness horrified me. Her sort of marriage was much worse than a lifetime of being alone. Being together that way would be the ultimate loneliness. What worried me most of all was the thought that at one point she and her husband had probably loved one another, had at least had the feelings that could bring me or anyone else my age to marriage. The possibility of love—or what I then thought of as love—vanishing, the thought of such a bleak marriage, made me understand, more than anything else could have, why so many of my friends were not only afraid of marriage but preferred anything at all to a commitment which might land them in that sort of horror.

Given the mess so many marriages are in, it is no wonder that a lot of people choose to live together on an uncommitted, tentative basis. I hope it will become clear in the following chapters that, while this may solve some problems, it closes off a fullness which is part of being human.

But there is another extreme, a more seductive one for those of us who believe that marriage is a good thing. That is the deification of marraige—the belief that marriage in and of itself is a redeeming thing which will save its participants, as if it were marriage itself which would save us and not something deeper which may be glimpsed at the depths of marriage. Even more insidious is the belief that we have fallen from some high standard to our current low estate. These are both forms of idolatry. They are understandably common in an age which seems full of threats to marriage and stable families, an age which finds the idea of a lifelong commitment impossible. But like all "golden age" beliefs (for example the belief that the novel, the church, urban life, or whatever subject you choose to throw into the proper space, once lived a healthy, holy, wholesome life totally unlike its current withered existence) these fancies are dangerously deceptive.

The danger lies in trying to recapture something which never existed, in trying to make modern marriages "as good as" something which never existed in the real world. A part of this danger lies in the fact that we will react by searching for a villain to blame when our false and nostalgic picture cannot be fulfilled; we will attack a perceived villain rather than criticize our own flawed vision and misplaced nostalgia.

We will see in the chapter on marriage as a sacrament whose focus has changed over the two millenia during which Christians have thought about it, that our recent romantic idea of love, the one which sees love as a deep infatuation so full of passion that it can hold its subjects together for life, is in fact both recent and very unrealistic. Marriage has been a radically different sort of commitment for most people in history; even in people whose initial approach was primarily an infatuated one the commitment must deepen to include something else, something more binding than attraction at the level of infatuation could ever be.

A difficulty which faces anyone trying to write a book about the subjects that cluster around marriage and sexuality is that values which have traditionally been attached to those subjects seem to be dissolving; and at the same time we must deal with the fact that our interpretation of those values has often been sentimental at best, and destructive at worst. We also have to try to understand the tendency of church people to accommodate themselves to the spirit of the age, an effort which has its positive side but which also leads to an uncritical attitude towards the latest received ideas which seem true because they are so much in the air. Those attitudes, questions, and difficulties which challenge the spirit of the age seem false precisely because they go against a grain which seems real, which has (like the eucharist, in a kind of blasphemous reversal) a real presence.

As in all other aspects of the Christian life our task is to fight our way from illusion to reality, from sleep to wakefulness, from drowsiness to alertness. This means dropping sentimental and nostalgic pictures of marriage and paying closer attention to what marriage at its best and worst can be like. We must, on the one hand, be clear about what is wrong—and also what is right—about the current set of attitudes towards marriage, both the high expectations people have with regard to personal fulfillment and familial hope, and the limitations of a model based on infatuation, romance, and the myth of the family as a model of paradise in an imperfect world. But we must also be clear about what was wrong with the older contractual model, which too often saw marriage as something simply to be endured. It did, however, have this strength: it knew that will is an essential part of love, and that what we now feel and think is not always, or even often, the best guide to our future understanding.

Celibacy is also discussed in one chapter. This is because vowed celibacy and marriage have been a kind of dialectic in Catholic history—one helping to illuminate the other. In addition, both are vowed commitments. One good aspect of our present confusion is that marriage is no longer simply the expected thing. Christian marriage is no longer as easily confused with respectability as it was when both the church and marriage were unchallengeable institutions. It may be that Christian marriage will not really come into its own until it is seen as a radical choice, radical the way monasticism is. The assumptions of secular culture make it seem more radical every day.

A SACRAMENT IN HISTORY

ONE of the fascinating things about marriage is how variously it is viewed—for some as a goal to be aimed at, and something to be avoided by others; as a trap, or as an adult homecoming. At times it has been viewed as the place where passion can come to its fullest point of development, and at other times it has been viewed as a hindrance to honest passion. I imagine that for many people it has at different times in their lives been both: both the fact of vowing fidelity to the beloved, and the belief that love and a vow of fidelity can conflict, coexist with one another and make life difficult.

The difficulty is helpful, if painful. It can instruct us about the extremely complicated reality of marriage, passion, vowing, fidelity, and infidelity. All of these things mirror the relationship of the soul to God and the relationship of the Christian community to Christ. But this deepest level of marital reality is not all that marriage is, or all that it has been in history.

Marriage is the sacrament best understood by secular people because it is common to every nation and culture. It has not always been monogamous, and it has not always been freighted with the emo-

23

tional expectations which marriage in the modern West carries, but it has always involved a degree of strong commitment and the belief that marriage is (among other things) a necessary way of cementing the bonds which tie families together, both in the present and through the generations, and it is a place of protection for the children who are born to it. In most cultures it has been a way of uniting not only individual men and women but families, in a network which included mutual support and obligation. This has been joked about—"a family is the place that, when you go there, they have to take you in"—but behind the joke is a serious truth. (This truth is what lies behind most polygamy: a brother takes on the obligation of a dead brother as husband, father, and supporter. This was true in ancient Judaism and is true in parts of modern Africa. A missionary priest I talked with was bothered by John Paul's condemnation of polygamy during his African trip. "He doesn't understand how vital it is to some societies," he said. "Too many people in the West think of it as an indulgence or an exploitation of women, as if men were polygamous for the sake of sexual variety. Believe me, I know that a polygamous marriage is in every way more difficult than monogamy.")

Because marriage unites families in ways which may work out for good or ill, its contractual side has been emphasized more in most cultures than its covenantal side. This latter is a Jewish and Christian emphasis, which concentrates more on the individuals who make the marriage than upon marriage as a dynastic, familial thing. Because a marriage can at one and the same time be a contractual agreement which unites families and serves a primarily social and economic purpose, and can also serve spiritual and profoundly personal purposes, it is necessary to define what face of marriage we are talking about. Marriage as a personal and religious covenant concerns us when we think of our current understanding of the sacrament; but in tracing the development of the sacramental understanding of marriage it is important to pay some attention to the contractual and social face of marriage, because it has much to do with the way the church as well as the surrounding society have regarded marriage.

The definition of sacraments which many of us memorized as children was too restrictive: we were taught that it was "an outward sign, instituted by Christ to give grace." But this forced some extreme interpretations of scripture. The only clear New Testament sacraments—if institution by Christ, or mention in scripture, are made essential parts of the criteria by which we judge a sacrament to be one—are the eucharist and baptism, and possibly the anointing of the sick (which is mentioned in the letter of James). Things which are mentioned in scripture (the washing of the disciples' feet by Jesus, which we repeat on Holy Thursday) we do not regard as sacraments, and things which are not (ceremonies of marriage or ordination) we do. These can be said to have been foreshadowed by various events or sayings of Jesus', but they are not *clearly* scriptural, as baptism and the eucharist are. At various times in church history whole numbers of sacraments which we now regard as "sacramentals" were listed by theologians—they included the sign of the cross, the blessing of holy water, the consecration of a bishop, the taking of the tonsure, to name only a few.

A better definition of sacrament is the older and more comprehensive one offered by Peter Lombard, who in his *Sentences* wrote that a sacrament "is a sign of God's grace, and is such an image of invisible grace that it bears its likeness and exists as its cause." The idea that a sacrament is the cause of what it signifies is true of symbolically sacred actions in every culture. A marriage ceremony in any culture both signifies a profound change in social status and brings about that change; it acknowledges the fact that this couple's place in society has changed radically, and their relationship to their own past and their own future has taken an important new form.

Given this fact, it is interesting that a religious wedding ceremony was not at all usual in the Catholic Church for half of Catholic history. The now common celebration of a church ceremony began to become common only in the eleventh century. According to John Martos, whose book *Doors to the Sacred* is an excellent history of the sacraments, "It

gradually became customary to hold weddings near a church, so that the newly married couple could go inside immediately afterward to obtain the priest's blessing. Eventually this developed into a wedding ceremony that was peformed at the church door and was followed by a nuptial mass inside the church during which the marriage was blessed. At the beginning of this development the clergy were present at the ceremony only as official witnesses and to give the required blessing, but as the years progressed priests began to assume some of the functions once relegated to the guardians and spouses themselves, and many of the once secular customs in the wedding ceremony became part of an ecclesiastical wedding ritual."

This could be seen as a clerical co-opting of a lay privilege, but there were many good reasons for the increasing ecclesiastical involvement, and some of today's canon law reflects them. For example, questions about the free consent of the bride and the groom, and about whether any other marriage has been contracted, make sense. They may seem insulting to those who have, of course, come honestly to the ceremony. But we have the formal and public ceremony in part because there were people (men, mainly) who contracted more than one marriage, keeping the others secret; and there were families who, for reasons of gain, would force their children into profitable marriage. The abuse of more than one secret marriage could be eliminated by the

requirement that marriage be done in front of the
community, and eventually recorded. The requirement that the parties affirm that their marriage was
entered freely put the church in the decent position
of being a protector of personal freedom.

There is an interesting contrast between the
Eastern Orthodox and Roman Catholic attitudes
towards the theology of marriage. In the East, the
priest is considered the minister of the sacrament.
He is the one who, representing the church, brings
what could be seen as the secular decision to marry
into the circle of Christ's covenant and makes it a
Christian mystery. In the West, the couple who
marry are the ministers of the sacrament, and the
church witnesses their decision. In both cases, the
questions of what consititutes a valid marriage, and
under what circumstances it can be said that a marriage does not exist, are part of canon law. This
made sense when the church was the ordinary
minister of marriage, but it can be asked whether
canon law as a parallel legal system makes good
Christian sense, or whether (at the very least) its
legalism should not be replaced by another vision of
what marriage is to be between Christians.

In trying to see marriage as a Christian reality we
must be aware of its history, which includes an in-
credible spread of attitudes. Marriage has been seen
as a contract between families, presided over in
whatever ceremonies there were by the fathers or
guardians of the families involved. It was seen first

as a secular agreement which had, for Christians, a sacramental depth because of the relationship between Christ and the church; and later it was seen as a specifically sacramental reality which had, almost accidentally, a secular resonance. There is a similar shift from an emphasis on contractual agreements between particular parties and (equally if not more important) particular families, to a covenant freely entered into in love by two individuals, sometimes with and sometimes without the consent of the families who gave the bride and groom their birth and raising. At one end of the spectrum the agreement of the parties was seen as the "matter" of the sacrament, the material thing which made it a sacrament; at the other end the fact of sexual intercourse was seen as the thing which made marriage an irrevocable fact. The shifts from contract to covenant, from a social and communal emphasis to a personal one, from one which stresses social obligation to one which stresses personal engagement and growth, are all important, and are not necessarily conflicting, though they sometimes are. And on top of all this is the fact Martos alludes to: that there was no single church ritual and no solid requirement that marriages be celebrated as a sacrament, like one of the other official sacraments, until rather late. There were, similarly, no uniform standards of canon law regarding marriage. There were times when it was considered acceptable for a Christian to divorce his wife and remarry for reasons which are no longer accepted in canon law. From country to country and century to century the reasons for disolving a marriage varied. A fourth century Greek Catholic could be admitted to communion, having remarried while his first wife was still alive, while a twentieth century Catholic whose misfortune it was to be born under current canon law could be kept from receiving the Body and Blood of Christ. All of this has been done in the name of the sacred character of a sacrament whose matter as defined in current canon law—sexual intercourse—was once commonly held to be almost always venially sinful. This comon attitude of moral theologians had to be carefully worked out, and eventually it worked its way out of the system altogether. Sex itself was not considered evil—the rejection of gnosticism and particularly of the Manichean heresy ruled that out. But the human heart was considered so corrupt that sex would almost always involve the parties engaged in lovemaking in such a thoroughly distracting paroxysm of desire that venial sin was held to be practically unavoidable. This attitude came into the church from pagan philosophy via Augustine—it was thoroughly un-Jewish—and it effectively ended when the rhythm method was accepted as licit. That acceptance meant that there were legitimate non-procreative uses for sex (a fact which was not news to happily married couples).

It is important to see this variety of attitudes towards canon law, the nature of the sacrament, and what constitutes the matter of the sacrament; it is especially interesting to see that what the church now accepts as the matter—the thing which makes it a sacrament—of the sacrament of marriage was once considered sinful. This is not to say that the history of marriage as a sacrament is simply a mess, although one could be forgiven for thinking that. It *is* a mess, but it is not *simply* a mess. The fact is that a close look at the history of anything reveals a mess, which is why we come up with convenient myths to make history more like a simple story than it possibly could be. (To take one example, the image of Luther striding towards the Wittenberg Cathedral door with a hammer in one hand and the ninety-five theses in the other as a crowd looks on in awe has been a Protestant icon; in fact he probably had to look for space, since the posting of theses on church doors was a common way of announcing debates in renaissance Europe.)

Early Christian attitudes towards marriage and sexuality were formed, as are ours, by the society and emotional climate of the time. Christians were negative about sex, but not nearly so negative as the stoics, the neoplatonists, or the gnostics who thought of sex not as mildly sinful, which would have been bad enough, but as a trap for the spirit, a binding and evil thing in which no wise man could be involved. Every society with which Christians dealt left a mark on the Christian tradition, including the way Christian tradition regarded sex. Christianity was stuck with some bad ideas as a result; but it was kept from some truly terrible ideas by the force of its own revelation. In his book, *St. Thomas Aquinas,* G.K. Chesterton made an excellent point about the way in which a tradition can save the church from moving too rapidly or in a radical extreme direction:

It was precisely the creed and dogma that saved the sanity of the world. These people generally propose an alternative religion of intuition and feeling. If, in the really Dark Ages, there had been a religion of feeling, it would have been a religion of black and suicidal feeling. It was the rigid creed that resisted the rush of suicidal feeling. The critics of asceticism are probably right in supposing that many a Western Hermit did *feel* rather like an Eastern fakir. But he could not really *think* like an Eastern fakir; because he was an orthodox Catholic. And what kept his thought in touch with healthier and more humanistic thought was simply and solely the Dogma. He could not deny that a good God had created the normal and natural world; he could not say that the devil had made the world; because he was not a Manichee. A thousand enthusiasts for celibacy, in the day of the great rush to the desert or the cloister, might have called marriage a sin, if they had only considered their individual ideals, in the modern manner, and their own immediate feelings about marriage.

If you begin with the idea that God's creation, with everything creation involves, is essentialy good, it is impossible to call sex evil. The most that can be said is that our fallen hearts are capable of turning a good thing to bad—but this is because of our hearts, which can be transformed.

There were people, as Chesterton points out, who would like to have made more negative pronouncements about sex, but Christian tradition, based in a scriptural understanding of life, would not allow it. It is important when looking from our modern point of view at previous Christian attitudes towards sex—or anything else—to consider what were the alternative ideas at the time. With what other attitudes towards sex and marriage did the Christian attitude contend? One thing which this can teach us is that there is something relative about the judgments which have been made about ethical and moral questions in every age. This bothers people who want simple and permanent rules for living. Not that there are no such guidelines at all—the ten commandments work now as well as ever, and the beatitudes (which are, like the commandments, more than rules) can't be improved on, or relativized away. These central statements of our tradition reflect an attitude towards our relationship to God which is permanent. The problem comes when we try to give final, definitive form to our interpretations of such permanently valid guidelines. The Holy Office is as limited in time and understanding as any group of rabbis, priests, or philosophers ever was. The standards which have been applied by those in authority have changed over the years. This fact, when pointed out, looks like a threat to the faith, at least to people who believe that those in authority must always be right if their authority is to mean anything at all. And they have a legitimate worry, because of the modern tendency to believe that our ways of seeing the world are essentially more clear-headed, enlightened, and basically *right* than the attitude of previous ages.

But the Christian tradition, with all of its shifts in understanding and occasional contradictions, has in fact held to several central tenets where marriage is concerned. Marriage is sacramental—a participation in the mystery of Christ. It is meant to be a perma-nent commitment. (The various exceptions made in the history of canon law show this, in a back-handed way; they are attempts to look for excep-tions to what is assumed to be the rule.) And, as the church reflected on marriage, over the centuries sex came to be seen as essential to the sacrament's holiness. So did the freedom of the participants: marriage was not allowed for family gain or dynastic power. As Chesterton's quote shows, the church's traditional understanding often made itself felt by going against the grain of the understanding common to an age. This certainly continues to be true: Christian marriage stands as a counter-sign in an age obsessed with individualism, merely personal fulfillment, and a lack of care for life at its beginning and its end.

HAVING FAMILIES

I KNOW couples who are waiting until the time is right for children, and I know other couples who have decided not to have children at all. In every case the reasons sound good, and it is certainly right that people determined never to have children (so much so that it forms an important topic of conversation for them) should not have children. A recent poll says that most American women do not consider children "essential to a good marriage." (The phrasing bothers me—*essential* doesn't mean the same thing as *important*, and not even the most conservative Thomistic theologian would argue that children are essential to a marriage.)

Something else is happening, and it is related to the choice to wait for children until the time is ripe, or not to have them at all. The past few years have seen the Attempted Perfect Family begin to crawl ashore; the next phase is an imagined cultural evolution which includes the Death of Patriarchy and the Emergence of the Senisitive Male. (Could our grandparents have imagined Woody Allen and Dustin Hoffman as heroic types, worthy of emulation?) The Attempted Perfect Family is one in which

36

the couple spend a lot of time working on their relationship, they have two children (three at the outside), eat carefully, and worry a lot about schools. The children already feel guilty about what is happening to the whales, and the odds are heavy that one little boy is named Jason.

I can't laugh at this too easily. I have two children, a girl and a boy, spaced two years apart. I worry about things like preservatives in food and whether the school is or isn't a decent place to be. I am not suggesting that people feed their children fatty foods or choose nerd names like Wilbur over fad names like Jason. I wouldn't want to be the patriarch of a brood of twenty, the results of every possible fertilization, all of them named after relatives because the relatives were there, like Everest, waiting to be named after. When any choice can be helpful to having a family it would be as irresponsible to avoid making it as it would be to avoid vaccination (since if it is God's will you will get polio, and if it isn't, you won't).

But it is wrong to make as much of choice and willing things as our society has. The difference between the Attempted Perfect Family and the older idea that you just aim at raising your children well and at making a good marriage is that the Attempted Perfect Family has everything to do with planning things right. If our relationship is right, the couple says, and our income level is right, and the children are in the right schools and we expose them to the right things at the right time—then we will have a decent family life. There are good concerns here, but we weight things one-sidedly when we make too much of planning. We run the risk of denying the importance of any larger claim, any involvement beyond the one I choose to have; and an exclusive concern for my rights, or my perception of my family's needs, can lead to a narrow vision—maybe a dangerously narrow one.

Genetically we are the products of people who got married when marriages were arranged and sometimes coerced, pregnancies were accidental, and there was always the best random factor of all: somebody with red hair liked something he saw in the eyes of a woman who was tall and thin and had a certain way of smiling. That is what got us this far. Planning has brought us much less, and our good intentions don't count for much. The fact that our air is terrible and our oceans are dying is the result of people "planning for growth." They weren't, of course, aware of other things, of balances which can't always be predicted and the sometimes unknowable effect of one system on another, seemingly unrelated system.

Which is precisely the point. In the course of living we are forced through times which involve us, more than we sometimes want to be involved, in coincidence, passion, the unexpected, calamity, randomness, wonder. We weren't expecting these moments, which is in a way part of their significance. These moments not only deepen us (as falling in love does, or the experience of the death of someone we love—these things take us far from our ordinary shallow concerns); they make up what we remember of our lives, and the lives of other people. Our planned moments fade next to the unplanned ones.

I am not suggesting that we do no planning and throw ourselves open to anything random; but I do worry about a view of life which absolutely excludes the unexpected, which cannot accept a reversal of fortune, an unplanned pregnancy, the loss of a job, or a change in school boundaries, without major upset.

The choice to have a family is difficult partly because it goes against our ordinary notions of choice and self-fulfillment. We come, in various ragged ways, from families. It is an arrangement few have been able to escape, and those who have don't seem the better for it. On the other hand, to revere family, to make an idol of it—a kind of cozy Victorian Christmas scene—is as wrong as it is to condemn the family for being oppressive and limiting, which in fact it often is. The family—like the person, like everything human—needs redeeming. The circumstances of being married and having a family open the possibility of redemption to us.

There is no surer way of forcing hospitality on

ourselves than to choose marriage and family. It is a vocation which means welcoming strangers. If you want to have children made in your own image and likeness you can try; and you might succeed in maiming them, and in creating monstrous problems for the victims of your love, if you don't in fact create monsters. The commitment demanded by marriage and parenthood calls for a love which cannot be impatient, and which is often not at all immediately satisfying. A good marriage, and good parenthood, are probably only appreciated over the long haul. I can say, after fifteen years of marriage and fourteen years of parenthood, that having a family is not at all what I expected. In almost every way it is at once better and more complicated than what I expected, but the point is that it is not what I counted on, and planning had almost nothing to do with what has become most important to me. Most of what I have learned in the process was learned without my knowing it until after the fact: I turn around after years of marriage and say, "So that's what it's like!"

This is fairly common. But our culture does not encourage an appreciation of slow learning, or commitments which are not immediately satisfying. Perhaps because of our ungodly emphasis on consumption we are encouraged to expect specific and obvious forms of satisfaction, and to feel deprived when we don't get what we expect. Our culture is opposed to the understandings which are needed to sustain families. The individualism and emphasis on self-fulfillment which are part of the air we breathe don't allow for the commitment a family demands of us.

Families are complicated, with patches of darkness as well as moments of light. As we grow into maturity we go through a process of resenting some of what our parents have done to us—usually they did what they did in the complicated way love leads us, meaning well and screwing up. Then, when we have our own children and make our own mistakes, we learn to forgive our parents, fully aware that we will give our own children much to forgive. There is no sure way to do everything right. We know this, and know that we have an obligation to proceed along the uncertain and necessary path love leads us, because we know that part of our function is to pass on the best of what we have been given (however unfashionable that best might be with the childrens' peer group). This is not only something we must not feel guilty about; it is an essential part of the parents' vocation. You will make mistakes—everyone does—but if your main concern is not making mistakes you will run into the extremes of needing either to be (or at least seem) infallible, or of raising a self-indulgent and unruly mess. It is better to make it as clear as you can that what you try to hand on (and sometimes even impose) is done in the name of love, not to be too heavy-handed about it or to guide in such a way that you can count on creating a reaction—like the pacifist parents I heard of whose son was made to feel so guilty about wanting to play with toy guns that he grew up to join the Marines—and all the time hope that love and mutual forebearance and forgiveness will keep you together.

It isn't simple. The emotional atmosphere of the average family reunion is not entirely comfortable; sometimes it seems that we know one another too well. But there is a love there which is, however complicated, deep, and in all of history we haven't figured out a better way to keep going on.

FATHERHOOD

MY daughter Maria, the firstborn of our two children, was born at seven months. The first month of her life was a struggle to live. I remember seeing her for the first time through two panes of glass. She was fighting for air, she was frightfully small and vulnerable-looking, and I knew in an unexpected rush that I would die to keep her alive if I could. It was the fiercest feeling I had ever known. It was my first experience of fatherhood.

This was the late sixties, when communication was everything, and people were given to saying things like, "How can you love somebody if you can't *communicate*?" The only communication between me and Maria wasn't really communication at all, but an agony that she be alive, and she couldn't possibly have known that I felt that way. It took the bottom out of whatever love had meant up to that point.

Until I was a parent I thought I knew pretty clearly what love was like: you willed to do the right thing, even when you didn't feel like it, and of course you knew what the right thing was. Paying attention to one's relationship with the other person, sweet reason, and a certain amount of self-sacrifice would all come together to make love work. Equipped with these reasonable-seeming ideas, I got married. A few months of marriage to someone who was suddenly—unfairly, it seemed to me at the time—a stranger taught me, painfully, that the growth of a marriage is frequently a growth in the dark. Years later a friend complained that her brother and his lover were always observing and talking about their relationship. "That's like watching a radish grow," she said. I recognized the problem; it was an old friend.

I thought that having a child would be a natural development—and of course it was, but I expected it to feel the way I thought natural things should feel. I wanted being a father to dovetail smoothly with being a husband. That was, of course, as mistaken as my earlier belief that marriage would be a relatively smooth transition from the relationship Regina and I had before marriage to the one we had afterwards. Instead, marriage and fatherhood went off like depth charges and rearranged everything.

It takes a long time to learn that not needing to be at the center of your life is a relief, not a deprivation. The consoling thing about marriage is that this learning, if you've been lucky or, better, blessed, is done in concert with someone you like very much. One strained metaphor has marriage a kind of dance, in which both partners make a pattern larger than they could make by themselves, a pattern which depends on both of them and has a center all its own, where both husband and wife can grow. The metaphor has its truth: marriage is about the creation of a (God forgive me this California word) space, but the strain comes from the fact that this dance involves such funny elements as inconvenient lust, loud chewing noises, and being patient while someone finishes reading a novel in a bathroom you want to use. (I've noticed that the most poetic generalizations about marriage come from celibates and people whose mates are long dead.) In its best moments—they do happen once in awhile—marriage is a conspiracy between people who know and love one another; forgiveness, acceptance, and humor need to be there.

Parenthood involves all of this, but in some essential ways it is different. No matter who you are, you have a terrible preparation for marriage and parenthood. If you come from a family in which there was deep and generous love, as most of us do, or believe we do, the forms of that love were probably so specific and complicated that their importation into marriage is difficult at best. In addition, you are likely to marry someone whose background is different enough to make your meeting and mating a funny, painful process of understanding. Each of us comes to adulthood through a process which has as much to do with myth as with rationality. Children are little reverse Freudians, mixing up their images of father and mother with their image of God, and even the

children of athiests know for awhile that their parents
are divinely right. Some of the anger of adolescence
is the realization that parents, too, are often wrong
and need forgiving. This means that you must make
your own way; you really are stuck in a world you
never made. (Later you meet this merciful knowledge: given the way your most disastrous personal
choices have been mercifully corrected by the real
world, you understand that a world you could make
would be hell, compared to the world you did not,
thank God, make.)

All of this gives you some fellowship with
your parents. In the long run you are blessed and
wounded by the same things: love, with all its com-
plications, and the helplessness that is part of love.
Yeats begins his *Poem For My Daughter* by telling of
"the murderous innocence of the sea." Part of our
love is a fear for our children, which comes from the
realization that this "murderous innocence" is shin-
ing at the depth of a universe which is indifferent to
us; it would enliven or kill our children as easily as it
would a sparrow or a clam. The love of God sustains
it, but this is a love which can somehow encompass
Hiroshima, Shirley Temple, hornets, me, Bach, the
progress of leukemia, and the flesh of Christ. It isn't
something you can be on easy terms with. In this
kind of universe we are asked, when we marry or
have children, to take a step into the dark.

The risk husbands and wives take is as risky as any
radical choice, but at least husbands and wives know

one another well enough to have some sense, however limited, of what to expect of the other. Parenthood presents something more mysterious: you do not know who this one is, or will be. Husbands and wives grow and change, of course, and like parents learning who their children are they must learn to continue discovering each other. But they have begun by knowing something of the other; it seems less risky.

Having children is even stranger than taking a vow. As scary as it is to be so hopeful, or so blind, something in us says that it is profoundly right to be. You do not know what to expect; you know even less than you did about marriage. There is less possibility than there is in marriage for an end to the relationship: because you have fathered or mothered this other one, you are responsible for life. Husbands and wives find it possible to cut loose from one another; various degrees of pain may attend the process, but it can be done. It is harder to deny your relationship to your children, which goes even deeper than marriage. The yearning of parents for their offspring can be holy or demonic or a terrible combination of the two. I remember a man, drunk and angry, screaming and hammering on the door of a neighboring apartment. His terrified wife, inside with their daughter, had to call the police. They were divorced a few months before, and he wanted to see his daughter. His wife's fear was entirely reasonable, but his agony was real, and his wild mixing of emotional self-interest and the desire to see his daughter was frightening to everyone within the sound of his shouting.

Family ties are as strong as anything human, and nobody can be objective about them. Ulysses on his adventures is a domestic man whose whole urge is towards wife and child; Antigone's loyalty to her dead brother puts her in peril; Abraham's hope is placed in a son he is asked to kill. If Jesus were not the beloved son of God the Father, if something less personal were involved, his suffering, and ours, would mean less.

Whatever the love of God for humanity might be, it must be mirrored in the ferocity and pity of fatherhood. By pity I mean the compassion referred to by the psalmist, who says that God regards us lovingly, "as a father pitieth his children." The motherhood of God is plain in the way the Bible speaks of Wisdom, and in Julian of Norwich's references to the motherhood of Jesus. This is a necessary filling-in, but it may be that the idea of God's fatherhood is essential precisely because of the ambiguity of fatherhood. We do not carry children to term; we are not the physical center, as mothers are, when our children are very young. We do not seem to be central, as mothers must be; but children could not exist without us. We love them, but our love is not necessary in any obvious way.

For that matter, there is nothing obviously welcoming or good about the universe we encounter daily. The weakness and vulnerability of fatherhood are the great secrets. Images of power and strength have to give way to the life-giving breath, the still small voice which remains when the storm and fire have passed by. This is where creation begins. We are met by magic here, especially in early childhood, which is full of real magic and raw poetry. Here you get to see myth in the molten stage. I remember a night at dinner when Maria and Hugh, aged five and three, ignored me and Regina and, with chicken bones in their hands, took up a chant. Maria began, "Before they had sticks, they used bones." Hugh took it up: "I wave over the water with my magic bones, I fly over the water with my magic wings." They chanted that way for awhile, little sorcerers. Poets, too: Hugh, watching the fluid motion of a neighbor's cat, asked me if cats had bones. Another time, trying to imagine a time when he didn't exist—the idea offended him—he asked where he was when Regina and I were married. I told him he wasn't anywhere then, he didn't exist, and he said, "Yes I did. I climbed up inside God's head, I looked out of his eye, and saw you." As they grow, our place in their lives changes. Maria is approaching adolescence now, asking the hardest questions, the kind that don't have answers.

Our culture deprives too many men of fatherhood. I know men who leave home for work before their children are out of bed, and see them again for a few minutes before bed-time. This busyness is culturally sanctioned, and it may be economically necessary for some people, but it is not a good thing. One of the most heartening trends today is the willingness of couples to work less and spend more time with their families. For too long motherhood was considered a special vocation, while fatherhood was a part-time job. The main work of women was holding the family together and raising the children. Fathers were there to give advice and earn money to keep the family enterprise going, but their real work, their important function, was to serve as stockbrokers or linemen, journalists, electricians, workers, lawyers . . . . Fathers had careers, while mothers did the holy work of caring for families. Feminism has helped to show the limitations of this approach to having families, and in the process more men are realizing that fatherhood is, or should be, as much a vocation and responsibility as motherhood is.

I grew up with seven younger brothers and sisters, but as an older brother I never saw children the way I see them as a father, perhaps because my solidarity was necessarily with other children. Parents were alien, frequently baffling. We knew they loved us and that we could depend on them; we also spent a lot of time trying to outwit them. The idea that my father, with his hairy hands and bristly face, had ever been a child never occurred to me as a serious possibility. He told us stories about his childhood, but he also told us stories about imaginary kingdoms, and I think his childhood was as fascinating and unreal to us as the magic ships and castles and gardens he told us about. Now I tell my children stories. I remember listening to them, and think of my father.

A friend of mine says that the ultimate ethical question is, what will you teach your children? What will you hand on? The poet Wendell Berry has suggested that the most radical thing a person can do is raise a family well. I realize that what I want to hand on to my children may not be what they get from me. The most I can do is try to understand them, let them know what matters to me and why it matters, love them, and while they are young enough to need leading, lead them the right way. Trying to be clear about these things I look at my children and have a sudden sharp memory of a moment when I was very small. I was holding my father's hand as we crossed the street. His hand felt large in mine, and the veins that stood out on the back of his hand were soft. As we crossed the street I pressed down on the veins on the back of my father's hand and found their softness reassuring. I hoped he didn't notice, because it seemed like a silly thing to do; but someday I hoped I would have hands like his.

GETTING ALONG

THERE is one scary central truth about being married: not much of the advice you get (and you get plenty) will be of any help. There are things about marriage that I would like to have known before I was married, but I really can't blame anyone for not teaching me—I am not sure I would have been able to hear and understand them at the time. One thing which has become clear to me (as not much else has) is that there is an immense difference between knowing something intellectually, and truly knowing it. It is possible to know that something makes entirely good sense, and to live in a way which contradicts that sense.

So there will be no "how-to" instruction here, nothing about techniques or methods. Books which treat bodies, and therefore souls, as a kind of real estate, or souls, and therefore bodies, as rooms which can be rearranged at will, ought to be distrusted. All I can do here is discuss some difficulties which are involved in living together as married people do, and hope that they make some sense. Learning to live together involves difficult growth. It is possible to make an easy peace in which one person dies because the other is allowed to dominate, or one person is diminished while the other blossoms.

This combination of growth and diminishing is frequently associated with work and careers. It is, of course, a deeper thing than that, but work has become an important and sometimes divisive issue in many marriages.

The "traditional" marriage has been caricatured as an arrangement in which women simply subordinated themselves to their husbands' careers, assuming that their main work was to support and enhance whatever choices their husbands chose to make. It's been pointed out that this was the pattern only for the upper economic strata, and even at that it was hardly ancient: in medieval and ancient societies, as well as in many tribal cultures, women were an essential part of economic life. This is not to say that ancient and tribal patterns were an unmixed blessing for women—far from it. But the model home of our most sentimental myths, in which the husband was the one with a career, who made money out in the world while his wife raised the children, is not only not ancient; it is relatively recent, and already on the way out. Today it is an economic luxury to have one adult at home all of the time.

That model was wrong not only because it demanded the subordination of feminine potential to male ambitions. It also deprived fathers of fatherhood. Too many men thought of being a parent as something they did best by providing money and advice; they did a kind of coaching at the end of the day or on weekends. Their presence was not obligatory; it was a sort of gift to the family. Mothers were the heavy presences, the ones who really had to be there.

The situation now is a split one: it involves options which seem to compound everything wrong with the past, and others which offer the possibility of a better way of being together and raising children.

There are people to whom a career is terribly important. They include as many women now as men, and families are being planned around the careers of both parents, rather than the career of the one parent who is providentially equipped with a helpmate to make his single career go smoothly. The great problem with this is that a lot of children are being shunted into daycare centers, where they are raised by "professional, caring people" and picked up in the evening by tired parents who spend as much of the rest of the day as they can being a family together. This is often an economic necessity, and insofar as it is really necessary it is important for families to deal with it well. But where it is not seen as an economic necessity but as a good and sufficient way of being parents, something might be missing.

I don't want a return to the old days. It doesn't matter which parent is there for the child most of the time, but the idea that one parent (not someone whose paid job it is to be a child-keeper) ought to be there for the child is not a bad one. Again, there are many situations in which this is simply not possible, and there are daycare centers which are extremely well-run, by people whose presence in the lives of children is a good thing. But the career of the individual parent, or of both parents, should never be the center of a marriage. Some couples, recognizing this, have managed to work at half-time jobs, so that fathers and mothers have more time with their children. Some mothers who have career opportunities which their husbands lack have been lucky enough—or perceptive enough—to marry men who understand that there is nothing at all wrong (and certainly there is nothing unnatural) about their spending the day with young children and a home which needs tending.

There are two points of view about work which make a difference to the place it assumes in the life of a family. One sees work as the thing which defines a person. Women and men are defined according to their careers and find their identities at work. (Think of the way we place friends when talking about them to people who don't know them: "He's a journalist. . . she's a lawyer"—as if this said anything really significant about another human being. What do we imagine we learn in that sort of exchange? And of course women are frequently asked "Do you work?" This means, of course, are you earning money by being paid for labor of some sort outside the home? Or are you—as too many women reply—"just a housewife?")

There is another point of view. It is far from common but it is more frequent now, even in these hard economic times, than it was in previous generations. That is one which sees the work one does for money and social status as only part of life, far from the most important part. There is a larger human enterprise and a more important work, which involves us in family, friendship, and forms of endeavor which are not necessarily profitable in monetary terms. Some couples have taken work which pays less but makes more personal sense than the jobs they held before, and some companies and academic institutions allow shared work plans, so that couples can share a job and spend more time with their children or at forms of work which are not necessarily profitable in monetary terms, but which matter personally and spiritually. Some companies have provided daycare on the premises, an arrangement which allows parents to see their small children during the day, and there are companies which provide not only maternity but paternity leaves to employees. A hard economy may force workers to place the demand for such changes behind the need for adequate wages and work assurances. That would be understandable, but truly regrettable.

I mention economic matters at the start of a chapter on getting along in marriage for two reasons.

One is that money and money-related problems are frequently named sources of tension in marriage, and disagreements over money surface in a great many divorce cases. It is important to discuss the values we attach to career and money before marriage. I know of one man who was content to work at a relatively low-paying job which pleased him. His wife, to put it nearly as simply as she did, wanted more money in her life and left him. I think he's well rid of her, but it is a shame that this issue couldn't have been dealt with before the mistake of a premature marriage made it so painful. Even for couples who have a healthier, less grasping attitude towards money—couples who are willing to live simply—security and the fear of not having enough can become obsessive, especially in hard times. I realize that this sounds very unrealistic, but the most important thing for couples to realize is that despite all of their natural worries, from a Christian point of view the correct attitude towards money is that it really does not matter. If you have what you need—and this does not necessarily mean what you want—you have enough.

Another reason I mention economic matters at the start is the fact that the culture which our economic system gives us has a direct bearing on daily life in marriage. Husbands and wives who work apart for most of a day (whether the husband is in one office or workplace and the wife at another, or wife works at home with children while the husband is away) come to one another in the evening having lived through two different days, each day with its own set of concerns, annoyances, successes, and disappointments. One may be eager to talk, while the other might simply want to relax and be left alone. Each expects his or her needs to be met, and feels resentful when the other's concerns are entirely different and don't mesh in any way with those of the husband or wife. This is easy enough to see, but in concrete reality it causes all sorts of hurt feelings, misunderstandings, and feelings of rejection which carry over into other areas of common life. This is not as likely to happen when people work together on some common task (though that will carry its own set of problems), or where schedules and the sort of work each person does are similar. But this is not the way most couples live, and a good deal of understanding, forbearance, and the occasional sacrifice of one's own desires—sometimes it is more than occasional—are necessary to make it through this aspect of marriage.

This problem points to something which married people have to learn sooner or later, and that is that there is a desire and a need for solitude which is as profound as the need for intimacy. Husbands and wives may feel the need for one or the other at different, sometimes conflicting times.

One important thing to remember about marriage, one which contradicts almost all of the trends in popular culture, is that it is *not* primarily about mutual needs being met. This has important practical consequences. It is important, for instance, not to resent the fact that a momentary desire is frustrated by the fact that your partner's mind is elsewhere. If your partner's mind is constantly elsewhere, that *is* worth discussing—but the fact that one of you needs companionship when the other needs privacy ought not to become an issue unless the privacy becomes constant isolation and fear of intimacy, or the need for companionship becomes smothering. There is a balance between solitude and companionship which is important not only in marriage but in every area of life. By solitude I don't mean the time we take alone to read or listen to records, though the need for that sort of privacy is important; I mean the time in undistracted silence which allows us to pray and to learn who we are before God, a time in which the masks and defenses we use socially can dissolve because in solitude they are useless, and they feel too heavy and hypocritical to be borne. What we learn in solitude can help us when we are with others, and we take what we learn there into solitude again. We lose ourselves when we allow the expectations of other people to determine the way we are with them; we put on airs, act a role, and forget oursevles. There is a Buddhist maxim which applies to honesty in marriage as it does to honesty in our relationship with anyone: we should act when we are with others as we would if we were alone, and we should act when we are alone as if we were with others. This singleness is close to what Kierkegaard meant when he said that purity of heart is to will one thing.

But there is a kind of honesty which can be destructive and unkind, even manipulative and, in a subtle way, coercive. In a particular moment it is kinder to feign interest than to be honestly bored; and if such a moment is not seen through, so much the better. If it is, it is best for the partner to understand it as an act of kindness rather than resent it as a hyprocritical pretense.

One of the most subtle and unpleasant difficulties which can arise in a marriage is the need of one person to dominate the other. This is not, of course, peculiar to marriage. It can happen in religious communities, in business organizations, in clubs; and it seems to be the basis of most of what we consider political. But it takes its most intimate form in marriage, and because married people know one another so well—a knowledge which includes the knowledge of weaknesses and soft spots, fears and hopes—it can be most wounding there. It is terrible when a husband or wife uses the other to prove himself or herself right or dominant (which, in the perverse dialectic that marriage at its worst can become, comes to the same thing). An important lesson for people to learn early on in marriage is that *you do not need to be right.*

Which is to say, you lose nothing at all if you are wrong. This goes against the grain, a grain which is reinforced at every turn and which was established in us at an infantile level. We never seem to outgrow it. People who have been involved in hot and passionate arguments—most of us, in other words—are aware that what might really have begun as an honest difference of opinion over the right course to take on any given issue quickly leaves that level and becomes a contest of wills which has very little to do with the truth or falsehood of your original point. There are disagreements worth having, but they should not be pursued passionately; the arguments which you must have ought to be urged quietly, and not in an atmosphere of heavy contention. This is easy to suggest as a wise course of action, and very difficult to achieve. What happens more often is that husbands and wives argue, push the argument to absurd and petty extremes, and then feel stupid when they have enough time to reflect on their own pettiness. Apology at this point often takes the form of "I was wrong, but . . . ." We try to salvage whatever shards of being right we can from a stupid battlefield, and the person who manages to walk away holding most of the fragments wins a contest which should never have been entered.

This has its analogue in other places, as I said above. Office politics usually has nothing to do with what the office is supposed to be about, and the politics of religious communities can be every bit as absurd as any office politics, or as absurd as the politics of marriage. But it is particularly painful and

sad when this happens to people who are supposed
to show the most intimate and vulnerable tenderness
to one another; and hardened hearts in marriage
have a more obviously ugly reality to deal with than
the situation which is faced by people who can
excuse their hardheartedness on the job by pointing
to the stupidity of the institution they are working
for. It is true that marriage is often called an institution; but its reality is not, like a job, one which can be
begun or left at will without too many consequences
(other than economic ones). Two people are involved at the depths of their hearts—two people at
least. Where children are involved, as they usually
are, the reality of marriage is a surrounding and protective thing, or something which hurts them, or a
combination of the two. The love of married people
is a freeing thing, a liberty unlike any other on this
planet, when it exists in its fullness. When the need
to be right (which has absolutely nothing to do with
any love for the truth of a particular situation) or any
other form of dominance prevails, the vocation
which involves allowing the other to be free is
betrayed.

The love of husbands and wives, like the love
parents have for children, can be a way of affirming
the self and shoring up the ego. Or it can be a profound affirmation of the other person at a depth
which is close to the moment of God's creation.
Somewhere Augustine wrote that love says to the

beloved: "Be." The attempt to make the loved one like ourselves, or to make the loved one be the way we want him or her to be, is not love at all. True love, real compassion, means a love for the other as he or she *is*; and this is an acceptance of mystery, because we don't know what the other is, or who the other is, without an attentiveness which doesn't try to change the other or fix the other up, but can simply be in the presence of the other, gratefully. It is the easiest thing in the world to betray the privilege we have to be this way with one another.

In marriage one form this betrayal can take is an attempt to counterfeit something which matters very much: there is a strength which married people can give to one another. Each of us has moral, spiritual, and personal uncertainties, and where one wavers the other can provide help. But we dislike our vulnerability: to admit that we need help and guidance is to show that we are not in charge of our lives, we are not complete in ourselves. If we can find the strength we need to find, it is something which requires the help of another; we cannot draw it out of ourselves at will, as if we were clear about our own needs and directions. There are moments (and days, and months, and years) when we do not know what we ought to do, or what we ought to be. These times of uncertainty aren't always times when the best help will come from husband or wife, but some help certainly will—or could, if we were able to articulate our needs without fear of revealing the vulnerability we all fear so greatly. To reveal that vulnerability can mean that we ask someone else to be responsible for areas of our life which we are in the dark about—not ultimately responsible (because ultimate responsibility lies with us) but responsible for showing us, in the knowledge the other has of us, what we may not be able to see ourselves, because we can be blinded by our own pictures of ourself, our own self-image.

I realize that this sounds very articulate, as if people sit around hashing these things out, talking them through, getting them straight in words. That isn't the way it usually works. Someone's particular hurt might exist below the level of words, and will have to be healed there. It can be healed silently, by compassion. Saint Francis of Assisi said that he was repelled by lepers, but then by the grace of God he "entered into the pain of their hearts." This is what compassion is—suffering with the other, going through what the other goes through without any remove, without a protecting distance. Hard as it is for a wordy man like me to admit, it has nothing to do with words. I once spent a few days in the company of a man who was not very bright, intellectually; his goodness was a healing thing. He was whole-heartedly good and prayerful as very few people are. Words may be involved in the process of what we are called to offer one another, but the right words, or the appearance of the right emotions and attitudes (in other words, our too-easily offered counterfeits of concern), are not the point.

We are called to be compassionate. It is harder to counterfeit compassion in marriage than anywhere else. In marriage people know one another so well that they can hurt and heal more deeply than anyone else—look at the happiest marriages and the most miserable break-ups. But this works in very complicated ways: look at the little forms of one-upsmanship that happen in very good marriages, and at the charity which attends some divorces.

We fear both vulnerability and strength because the vulnerability we really have, whether we want to admit it or not, forces us to acknowledge that we do not have the power to build ourselves in our own image. This ought to lead us to thank God; but to relinquish the self is painful. It is (as some of Jesus' sayings indicate) a kind of death. We fear the strength we are called to because it makes us responsible for another's pain as well as our own. We would rather have strength spent in building up the self, not the other. In weakness we find that there really is help which is there for us, that we can be strong only when we know our weakness in its depths. When we try to be strong and self-sufficient, we find that we are weak, that our strength is not only not something which exists for ourselves or which we can draw at will out of ourselves, but it does not exist *in* the self. It comes from a source which is both in us, and beyond us.

Much of the truth we need to know about marriage is symbolized in sex, which tells us about passion, vulnerability, attentiveness, care, and need. Sex is, everyone acknowledges (well, almost everyone) an important part of marriage. There are all sorts of books about sexual technique, most of them useless because they are filled with things which you could arrive at without their help, using your imagination.

The problem is that technique won't make much of a difference when one of the partners is cool to lovemaking; and when both partners are willing to talk about sex books won't be necessary. (If they find that sex is a source of frequent controversy, a third party might be more helpful than a book. Taking a cue from the ancient Irish legal code, the right procedure here would probably have to begin with an agreement on who might be an objective third party. At this point I'll step out of the room.)

Sex is the matter of the sacrament of marriage, which is to say that in Catholic terms it is the thing which makes a sacrament what it is. Just as we hope that a Mass will be more than merely valid, we hope that a marriage will be more than merely licit. Sex, as a sacramental reality, ought to be good, and not too solemn. If it isn't pleasure, if it isn't enjoyed, something is wrong. And if something is wrong, it could help to talk about it. The idea that most of us grew up with—that sex shouldn't be talked about—might be good advice for public dinner parties, but if married people can't talk about sex with one another they will almost certainly suffer from that lack.

It is important, however, not to separate sex from the rest of marriage. While sex is an important part of getting along together, and ought to be at least a very pleasant experience, it is also a sign of the deeper aspects of love. It is a pledge of something that matters more than pleasure. In lovemaking people become vulnerable; their nakedness is both a sign of openness and need; their tenderness and passion represent a love and commitment which, if it does not exist outside the moment of lovemaking, makes sex a lie. If in every area of marriage except for sex things are going along well, sex will probably eventually come around and be all right, too, especially if the couple are willing to talk about it with one another (this doesn't mean arguing about it, but making feelings and wishes known, knowing that one's own feelings and wishes are as limited and blind as are the other's). If, on the other hand, people are great in bed together, but in other areas of marriage there is a great deal of pettiness and selfishness and manipulation, the marriage is in serious trouble and in serious need of help.

This ought to be obvious, but it might not be in a culture which often suffers from what C.S. Lewis once described as a dangerous form of "sex-worship," something he distinguished from a normal and healthy appreciation of eros. People who separate sex from the rest of their lives, who regard it as an area of life within which they will find or lose themseves, who separate sex from marriage and companionship, make it a cheerless and dutiful thing, a therapeutic necessity. There is something joyless and desperate about sex in too many lives, and it comes from removing sex from the context it makes most sense in, the one where we know one another too well to let sex become (if I may put the word in, where it may seem incongruous) humorless.

Sex is obviously at the center of marriage, but sex does not equal sexual technique, or constant and obvious satisfaction. What sex signifies in marriage must be more than that. If it is not, the marriage is lacking something essential.

Communication—not only about sex but about everything of mutual concern—is terribly important. So is respect for the other's need for solitude and privacy, a respect precisely for the other's *otherness*. This is a respect for the fact that in each of us there is something that is alone before God. No one else has a right or claim to this place in us. It is a singleness which is the abode of mystery, the place of deepest contact with what each one of us, beyond the definitions given us by our families and friends and lovers and society, simply *is*. It can be shared to an extent, but not completely. We cannot demand total sharing, because it is not possible. We can only offer what we can offer, what we have at hand to offer.

The deeepest reaches of ourselves are not ours, and are not offerable.

The desire to make sex, or communication, or any other skill we might master the keystone to a successful marriage is an unfaithful one. We need to make our absolute need for God the center of marriage, as it needs to be the center of everything else.

THE SPIRITUALITY OF MARRIAGE

THERE have been many sentimental pictures of marriage and family life, and we are deluged with them at Christmas, on Mother's Day, and in sermons which occur off and on (like dandelions springing up in unexpected parts of the lawn) when the preacher can't think of anything else to talk about: the goodness of family life and the importance of having a good marriage are safe topics. There are church documents which speak of the home as "a church in miniature," and there is often the intimation that family and marriage are, in and of themselves, holy, sanctified, and full of grace.

C.S. Lewis wrote a short essay, "The Sermon and the Lunch" (it is reprinted in *God in the Dock*), which makes some very fine points about marriage and family life. "Since the Fall no organization or way of life whatever has a natural tendency to go right," he says. "The family...can be converted and redeemed, and will then become the channel of particular blessings and graces. But, like everything else that is human, it needs redemption. Unredeemed, it will produce only particular temptations, corruptions, and miseries. Charity begins at home:

so does uncharity." Lewis goes on to point out that the preservation of what we normally call love—natural affection, as opposed to real charity—is not enough: "Left to its natural bent affection becomes in the end greedy, naggingly solicitous, jealous, exacting, timorous. It suffers agony when its object is present. . . The greed to be loved is a fearful thing. Some of those who say (and almost with pride) that they live only for love come, at last, to live in incessant resentment." To the sentimental argument that home is a place where we can "be ourselves" Lewis answers that "what chiefly distinguishes domestic from public conversation is surely very often simply its downright rudeness. What distinguishes domestic behavior is often its selfishness, slovenliness, incivility—even brutality."

I begin by quoting Lewis because, as is so often the case with his writing, he is making good unsentimental sense here. The home, like all human institutions, needs redeeming. We should not assume that it is, as it is, a source of grace. It can instead be a battleground for the egos of everyone involved in it, more dangerous the more it is sentimentalized, because then the damage done to people is said to be done "for their own good," out of love; and this state of affairs can lead to the most complicated and intricate forms of guilt and resentment. One friend—perhaps she was quoting—defines the family as "a social unit which is dominated by the sickest member," and that picture is true of too many families to make her remark simply a joke.

To say that marriage is a sacrament means that it is a sign which signifies a reality at the same time that it helps to bring that reality about. But marriage is also a secular social reality. It would be easy to say that a Christian in this sense has a foot in both worlds, or that two realities, religious and secular, are involved here. This is true up to a point, but at the depths of marriage one reality is involved, and the other is a popular delusion. Secular marriage is a shadow of the reality, a dream from which we are called to awake, just as secular allegiances are at best precursors (where they aren't blasphemous imitations) of the obedience we are asked to give to God.

The sacramental aspect of Christianity begins with human givens, like being born, dying, and, in between, suffering, doing wrong, loving, being cleansed, eating, drinking, making love, and making such drastic choices as life-long mutual obligation to another person, and parenthood. These given things are not yet "sacramental," "holy," "redeemed;" they are all the sorts of events (the choices are themselves events) which mark the lives of most people. What Christians call "holy," "sacramental," "redeemed," is a presence which is hidden in the reality of the event and must be brought forth. It can begin to be brought forth when the real presence of Christ's living reality is detected where it was hidden before. Before revelation's light hit it the reality was two-dimensional; with the new light slanting in it is thrown into relief and is seen for the first time to be three-dimensional; and our lives, our relationships to those old realities, are suddenly deepened and renewed. This is what the sacraments call forth. We do not live in two orders of reality, the sacred and the profane, the religious and the secular. We live in one reality, and it has depths which are illuminated by the sacramental insight. To say that the word became flesh means that everything human—absolutely everything, including our shame and fear, any horror that we might feel when we see the worst aspects of our lives—is not only known by God, but is made a means of our salvation. What might have been a distraction, a way away from God, is not only pronounced good (as God calls all of creation at the beginning of Genesis) but is made a means of our salvation.

True love calls upon the beloved to be what the beloved is, at the depths of the beloved's being. But what does that mean? How do you allow another simply to be? Love can be a terrible thing, when we twist it as we so often do to fulfill what we feel are our needs. It can be the most manipulative thing in the world; it can reduce the other to nothing. Marriage can be an attempt to make the other into your own image, a blasphemous parody of God's relationship to each of us. It is not only in marriage and family that we do these things. They can happen in religious communities, and to a lesser but still terrible extent in classrooms and at work. But marriage and family are the most intimate places we know, the ones in which we are cut closest to the soul by what we receive or fail to receive, and in which we can bless or wound by giving or failing to give love. It is this closeness that any spirituality of marriage must address.

There is one sense in which there are really no special sorts of spirituality. Efforts to find a "lay spirituality" or a particular form of spirituality which is entirely appropriate to priests, religious, contemplative, married or single people, are finally self-defeating. So when I write about a spirituality of marriage I don't mean that what is said here does not apply at all to single people or vowed celibates or others. I believe that married people have much to learn from the monastery, and that their own spirituality will be less without contact with contemplative traditions.

Just as the sort of spirituality which has developed in monasteries can be helpful to people who don't live in them, so a spirituality which can disclose itself in marriage can be helpful to people who are not married. The spirituality which celibacy discloses has to do with the fact that each of us is finally alone before God. This aloneness is a fact; it is not something to be remedied or avoided. Insofar as we avoid it we create unhappiness. When we try to force our way into another's deepest aloneness, when we insist on knowing them at that depth, we violate them. It can't be done, and the attempt only causes suffering. (Jacobo Timerman wrote of his own experience of torture in Argentine prisons that the torturer seeks not to force the tortured person to reveal information, but rather to reveal himself.) To the degree that we avoid the fact of that essential aloneness or fail to accept if fully, we convert aloneness into loneliness.

One sort of wound which married people can inflict upon one another is to use marriage—which means specifically to use the other—to evade loneliness and heal it. Of course the companionship you can find in marriage is a helpful thing, and ordinary human loneliness is alleviated by it. But at times married people can demand that the other understand, heal, or satisfy at a depth which no other human being can reach. This is an invasion of the aloneness which is an essential part of being human; it is the central part of us, the place where God can meet us in our emptiness, and part of what we must learn in marriage is to respect that ultimate privacy in the other, because it is the place at which the other meets God most intimately.

The idea that we meet God primarily in solitude is something which goes against the grain. Many writers have challenged it on the grounds that we meet God most in our neighbor. The place we must find God, they would say, is in the thick of community, whether the community is the family, a religious community, or the community of our friends. The problem is that, while God is indeed to

be encountered here, unless we first open ourselves
to God in solitude our sensibility and mode of
understanding will be too cluttered to meet his
presence in community. We tend to sentimentalize
God; we make God a projection of our own deepest
needs and desires; we use a notion or picture of God
(or rather of our idea of God, since God cannot be
imagined or pictured in any but an idolatrous way) to
bolster the sense we want to have of ourselves or our
place in the lives of others. The one thing we cannot
do under this set of circumstances is encounter the
living God. In any community, including the family,
we find ourselves eager to protect the image we
have of ourselves, an image which we think we must
keep. We identify the self-image with the self, an
identification which is always false. A community
can reinforce this by accepting this projected self-
image as the truth about us; or it can challenge the
image, at which point we become defensive and try
to reinforce it with all of the energy we can bring to
the task. It is only in solitude that we can begin to
shed our armor—in solitude, or in sleep, where our
dreams may reveal our deepest desires and fears
and needs (and seeing them clearly can be uncomfortable). Our armor begins to drift away from us in
sleep; it can be seen from new angles, seen for what
it is. Our dreams are affected by the attitudes which
are part of our waking hours, and they are not free
of our compulsions and the tricks ego uses to defend
itself. But by revealing themselves in a dream-light

those compulsions can come to our attention for the
first time. It is also important, during the day, to pay
attention to our ordinary emotional reactions to
ordinary events: what is it that makes us impatient,
irritable, angry, or hurt? What part of us is really hurt
by these things—what part that matters? Self-
observation can make us aware of the infantile and
ego-centered quality of much of our emotional life.
Some spiritual directors have asked the people who
come to them to confess their thoughts—not just
their "bad thoughts," the unkind or lustful or greedy
or angry ones, but all of their most ordinary reactions. The reason for this is that even what we
ordinarily regard as innocent or ethical behavior can
be self-serving, and can reinforce the self we are asked to give up. In solitude, in the attempt to quiet the
soul, all sorts of odd and sometimes disturbing things
can surface. When we realize that they are part of
the defensiveness which keeps us from God and
from other people, the realization is uncomfortable;
but it does at least serve the purpose of warning us,
so that we can put those reactions in their place. In
solitude our armor begins to seem heavy and un-
necessary. We may not be free of it yet, but at least
we begin to get a sense of how imprisoned we are.
When we try to silence ourselves in the presence of
God—or rather when we pay attention to the fact
that we are in the presence of a God we cannot
know, the way we know other things—we learn how
unruly, how ungathered our perception is. What we

really are is revealed more clearly than it can be when we are with others.

John of the Cross said that when he went out to be with others he returned to solitude less a man than he was when he left it. This does not mean that we should spend all or most of our time alone; but it does mean that without alone-ness we will not know what it is we bring to others.

One thing we can learn from meditation is that what we ordinarily consider the self really is nothing. I don't mean that rhetorically, as if to say that what we ordinarily consider the self doesn't matter as much as we thought it did, or that it really is pretty silly. It really is nothing, it doesn't exist (except as the illusion little children sometimes have exists—that is, the belief that things which are closer to them are really larger, and things far away, like an airplane in the sky, are really small). As long as we think of what we regard as our self as something solid we place an obstacle between ourselves and truth. This is what I referred to earlier, when I wrote about the part of the self that feels wounded. When I am offended I am unlikely to ask seriously what it was in me that was hurt by the offense, unless I spend enough time in solitude and honest self-examination to pay attention to this sort of question. Ordinarily there is no real question of justice or injustice involved, but only wounded vanity. If I am accused of pride or arrogance, or of having done bad work, or of having missed an important and even obvious point, I am faced (once I get over the bad feeling of having been told whatever it was that gave me offense) with the fact that my critic may really be right, in which case my feeling of offense is the result of trying to hold on to a picture of myself which is at least flawed, if not downright false; or I may realize that the critic is simply wrong—but if I were sure of that, and not unwilling to let go of a self-image to see what the truth might be, then I would not feel wounded, any more than I would feel personally wronged by someone who insisted that the earth is flat or that two and two make five. We tend to identify our self with the constellation of feelings and desires we carry around with us, usually unaware of them until they are hurt, or until something puffs them up. When we are hurt because a fantasy of our own creation has the air let out of it and collapses (and this is a source of a good many of our most deeply felt wounds) then as painful as the experience might be, we really ought to be grateful. We have seen through something, and have a clearer vision of what we are not.

What we *are* is far more difficult to know. We are meant to reveal the image of God, but there is a long way from what we are now to that ultimate reality. My own feeling about real human identity is a scary one. It scares me, anyway. I have the strong suspicion that whatever it is that doesn't die in us, whatever our eternal self is or will be, it has very little to do with what we consider ourselves. Ordinary sleep can knock the stuffing out of ordinary waking identity, and a decent dose of sodium pentothal more or less eliminates it. What brain death does I can't imagine, but I find it difficult to believe that most of what seems like heavy baggage even now, most of what I think of as myself, will or ought to survive death. What am I left with? I don't know. The first letter of John says that we do not know what we will be, but we will see Christ as he is, and be like him. I don't think that, as most of us are, we can have any clear idea of what this means at all. Something is being brought to birth in us; it is growing and is being nurtured, unless we turn away from God completely. When it comes to fruition it will no doubt surprise us and delight us. But we are now in the relationship of the seed to the full-grown flower, or the newly conceived child to the adult, and have about as much real understanding.

The problem of identity in prayer and contemplation has been dealt with by Christian mystics and (in some fascinating detail) by Buddhist thinkers. What does it have to do with marriage?

A lot, I think. The armor that is part of ordinary living is something husbands and wives see through, to a certain extent. In marriage we come to be known as we are known nowhere else. This fact is enough to break up some marriages. When Paul says that our knowledge is now obscure, and we see ourselves "as in a darkened mirror," but "we will know as now we are known," he says that we will know ourselves as we are known by God. That is part of the goal, part of what will be revealed. In marriage we are known more intimately than we would like to be known, sometimes, because the knowing can pierce our armor. We are seen through by the one who loves us, and we are still loved.

When Paul compares marriage to the love Christ has for the church and the love the church has for Christ, this kind of knowing is involved. To be known in our weakness, fear, vulnerability, need, and emptiness, and still be loved, is wonderful. That love is grace-filled, and grace-bearing. But it can also be uncomfortable, because to accept that love means to accept the weakness and emptiness in ourselves. We know ourselves as we are known. It is a participation, however obscure, in the knowing Paul writes about, the knowing which takes us into the life of God. To be known as we are may be uncomfortable at first, but if it is accepted as it should be it is a cleansing thing, a means towards an honesty which cannot happen without it. It is possible for friends and members of a religious community to know one another deeply, but there is a depth to knowing which can happen only in marriage; or perhaps it would be more accurate to say that it happens rarely outside of the sort of intimacy marriage makes possible.

I said that this "being known" can break up marriages. To know someone intimately means that you can enter into the other's hurt, as if it were your own—you can be compassionate, can suffer with the other, accepting the other's darkness as you accept your own. You can also use that darkness, knowing the other's weaknesses. (Once I saw an old couple in a laundromat. The husband abused his wife verbally, insulting her, ordering her around, and she accepted her slave status, looking as unhappy as a human being can. It was a hideous thing to see, a picture of a kind of damnation. It was especially terrible because of their age. Not that a younger couple's horror story would be acceptable; but the thought that the lives of two old people were ending this way was, not tragic, since tragedy has its ennobling points, but literally hellish.) Even between couples whose life together is on the whole a good one, appreciative and attentive, there can be moments in which the other's weakness is used, and they are dangerous.

This first aspect of knowing and being known has to do with being on the knowing end, with knowing the other and accepting both the otherness of the other and the darkness, the emptiness and pain of the other, as your own, rather than using what we know to manipulate the other. When we meet any other human being at this level we can do only three things: we can be indifferent, we can be manipulative, or we can be compassionate. We are given the power to use and abuse, and the power to heal and forgive and suffer with, at one and the same time.

The other aspect of knowing and being known

involves the receiving end, the place where we are known. It has its own set of difficulties. The phenomenon of the man in his forties who leaves a wife of twenty years for a younger woman is, I think, often the case of a man who is uncomfortable with being known. What I mean is that the image you may want to have of yourself is not necessarily true—it is almost certainly not true, in fact. If someone knows you well enough to see you as you are, and another person (who doesn't know you nearly as well) believes the image you prefer to project, it will be easy to believe that the latter person understands you better than the former, because she confirms the picture you prefer to have of yourself. This feels like the truth, like understanding, when it is in fact the reinforcement of an illusion. To be known as you are can violate your imagined self, and the person who reinforces the imagined self makes you feel younger and more alive, because you are brought back freshly to the illusions of youth.

It is important to know how to be on the active end of knowing, and the passive end of being known, without violating the other or being too defensive about what gets known in the process. Humor is essential here, and gives a sense of proportion to our ordinary tendency to take ourselves very seriously (and this may be why so many of the best marriages—and the best religious communities—involve a lot of joking). In addition it is necessary to understand that there is as much tolerant affection in love as there is passion, and probably even more. For couples who are well-married there can even be the delightful discovery of passion at the depths of tolerant affection.

Remembering Lewis' caution, though, it is important to pay attention even to these good things without taking them for granted. Tolerant affection can degenerate into manipulative condescension, and passion can become physical selfishness.

The attention we need is developed by prayer. It is good for married couples and for families to pray together; it is probably essential, if you want your children to take prayer seriously at all. But prayer alone is more important than prayer together. We can be honest in solitary prayer as we can never be when we are with others. I don't mean to contrast honesty with dishonesty here, as if we were not honest in company. I mean to compare it to nakedness. Our being together is always, to some degree, clothed. That's proper and civilized. And we can't ever get away from it completely. Even after years of marriage people still communicate not only through words but through a kind of code done with the face, the attitude of the body, through silences and pauses. Absolute communication, one which dispenses with all of these things, is absolutely impossible. When we pray with others this layer of clothing will be present precisely because we are together.

The love we bring to others is not something we can simply will in a shallow way; it can't come into its fullness just because we want it to be there. If love is to be more than natural affection it will require silence and some solitude. The love we bring to one another from prayer is a reflection of the unconditional love God has for us, if it is a love which listens, first in silence, and then in the company of the other. It doesn't depend on the other being the one I want the other to be; the love which depends upon the fulfillment of personal expectations is not love, because it does not allow the other to exist as another person, but only as a means to personal fulfillment. If I "love" another person solely because the other meets my expectations, I have simply used the other as an emotional backscratcher. I have made a thing of another human being.

In marriage, as in no other sacrament, we are asked to accept another human being unconditionally, and this is one reason marriage is a model of Christ's relationship to the church. Jesus said very little about marriage, but the exchange in chapter 19 of Matthew's gospel is a rich one: "And Pharisees came up to him and tested him by asking, 'Is it lawful to divorce one's life for any cause?' He answered, 'Have you not read that he who made them from the beginning made them male and female, and said "For this reason a man shall leave his father and mother and be joined to his wife, and the two shall become one?" So they are no longer two but one.

What therefore God has joined together, let no man put asunder.' They said to him, 'Why then did Moses command one to give a certificate of divorce, and to put her away?' He said to them, 'For your hardness of heart Moses allowed you to divorce your wives, but from the beginning it was not so. And I say to you: whoever divorces his wife, except for unchastity, and marries another, commits adultery; and he who marries a divorced woman commits adultery.' The disciples said to him, 'If such is the case of a man with his wife, it is not expedient to marry.' But he said to them, 'Not all men can receive this precept, but only those to whom it is given. For there are eunuchs who have been so from birth, and there are eunuchs who have been made eunuchs by men, and there are eunuchs who have made themselves eunuchs for the sake of the kingdom of heaven. He who is able to receive this, let him receive it.'"

The dispute which the Pharisees brought to Jesus was a lively one. The great scholars Hillel and Shammai lived a few years before Jesus, and had widely differing views of divorce. Hillel was easy where divorce was concerned: the fact that a husband didn't like the way his soup was prepared was sufficient grounds for divorce, he felt. Shammai was much stricter and demanded grave cause before a divorce should be permitted. Jesus shows himself to be even stricter than Shammai here. He makes an interesting appeal: he goes beyond Moses to the way it was "in the beginning." He refers to the passages in Genesis which have to do with the creation of humanity, and with the need for the two to become one flesh. In Genesis the female is taken from the male, flesh of his flesh, and in a sense men and women thus become whole only when they are joined to one another again. There were myths current in the world Jesus and his hearers lived in (you can find one version in Plato) which spoke of a primordial human condition in which human beings contained both sexes in one body; they were cut apart and forced to seek the other half of themselves. In finding one another a man and woman "are no longer two but one." Marriage is a restoration of something true at the beginning, true of our most basic humanity. The possibility of ending marriage was allowed, Jesus said, "for your hardness of heart"—in other words, because you were incapable of living marriage as it should be lived (and here Jesus makes it clear that if a marriage ends it is not because it should, in the objective order of things, but because of an incapacity on our parts)—"but from the beginning it was not so." Only adultery, the most deliberate betrayal of the "two in one flesh," justifies divorce.

The disciples, on hearing Jesus' rather tough attitude towards divorce, conclude that "it is not expedient to marry." (I've always found this response funny, as if they were saying "if we can't bail out, the hell with it!") When Jesus responds that some have

made themselves eunuchs for the sake of the
kingdom, his words have been taken as a defense of
life-long consecrated celibacy. Scripture scholar
Quentin Quesnell suggests that it might instead refer
to those whose marriages have ended and who
refuse to remarry. They refuse to give up on the
other, or on the possibility of reconciliation. This
reading of the passage takes us back to the prophet
Hosea, who refused to abandon his prostitute wife,
but waited for her to return, willing to endure any
number of betrayals in the hope that eventually she
would come home to him. What is underscored here
is the Christian fact that we cannot abandon or give
up on anyone. The role of the good lover, the
faithful spouse, is to wait as God does. This willingness to assume that repentence and grace and
forgiveness and reconciliation are possible for any
one of us is an essential part of our relationship with
God, and of marriage. It is strange to think that marriage as a vocation may sometimes be witnessed to
best by those who have suffered from marital
breakup, but that may be so. It might strike us as
strange that God's relationship to us is sometimes
revealed more clearly in broken relationships than in
whole ones, but this is the story of redemption. We
are not at all what we are meant to be. In our
darkness we hurt one another and find our relationship to God shattered again and again. God's
presence can be revealed in the broken moments, a
waiting and forgiving presence.

Spirituality is not something which saves us, not a technique which works but rather a form of attention. It is essential not only to marriage but to all of the sacraments, to our whole life. A sacrament's grace does not impose itself on us like a mold, but can work only if we are predisposed to see what the sacrament means, what it calls us to. We must be ready to be transformed.

There is a way of hoping that membership in a church, participation in the sacraments, and ordinary moral behavior will save us. But we are called to transformation and new life. We can convert all the elements of our religion into a means of feeling certain emotions, waving certain flags, certifying ourselves as OK sorts—even though we know with Paul that the "good I would do, I do not do;" even though we know in our deepest selves that we are not what we are meant to be. Jesus will not impose his life on us. We must be ready to receive that life, to have the whole of the self made over. Marriage may be metaphorically a wonderful picture of the relationship between Christ and the church, but unless we can learn to receive one another as Jesus receives us the picture is distant, sentimental, and basically useless. It may take the shock of seeing a marriage in which the image of marriage is violated to make marriage clear to us. In Shusako Endo's brilliant novel, *Silence*, a man learns the depth of Christ's love only when he understands that Christ's love can accept even his own betrayal of it.

These things can be learned only if we are able to arrive at some sense of the distance between what we are and what we are called to be. The sort of spirituality which aims at making us feel good isn't spirituality at all, but a kind of novocain. The spirituality of marriage is as trying as any, sometimes. It involves responding to the spiritual demands of intimacy in a way which knows that intimacy is at once vital, and not the whole point; a way which knows that there are claims other people have on us which matter deeply, and that even those claims might have to be transcended. Thomas More knew that something mattered more than a continued existence with his family, and at the same time he knew to the point of agony exactly how much he was losing in taking the course he took.

Christian spirituality of any sort begins in specific circumstances (celibacy, marriage, the desert, a poor neighborhood, a monastery, a home) and points us towards the life revealed in Christ, in whom we live, the Word which is the universe's meaning. The depths of the word are known not through study (though that is important) but through experience, an experience which begins and ends in prayer. The spirituality of marriage emphasizes the attention we must pay to the infinite fullness of our vocation: we are to become sharers in a divinity which is manifested not only in ourselves alone, but in the person to whom we are pledged for life. It is both a test and a privilege to be on such intimate terms with divine raw material; and it has to be remembered that it is divine, it is not ours. "Do you not know that your body is a temple of the Holy Spirit within you, which you have from God? You are not your own; you were bought with a price. So glorify God in your body" (1 Cor. 6, 19-20). A spirituality which takes our divine vocation seriously must begin by respecting the solitude of the other, the holiness of that very otherness, or it will become a manipulative and coercive thing.

There is one more, very important thing which must be said about marriage, and that is the fact that just as marriage reflects the relationship of Christ to the church, so our parenthood reflects the relationships of God to each one of us. There is something helpless about the love parents have for their children. To know that helplessness is essential. It is a reflection of God's helpless love for us. Parents sometimes feel in their deepest selves and with a fierceness that doesn't attach to any other relationship the fact that they would die, if necessary, to give their children life. Perhaps this is felt most keenly when a child is suffering. (In angry moments I could say that God has no right to relate to us any other way, given what so many of us suffer.) This love is deeper than any emotion or feeling. There is no deeper love than the love which exists to allow the other to be. God pours his life out in Christ on the cross, so that we can be. There is a wonderful line in Thomas Aquinas' writing: "The good is diffusive of itself." Good cannot be contained. Our response to the love we have been given should be, in gratitude, to continue it.

MARRIAGE AND CELIBACY

FOR years celibate Catholic priests have spoken to married Catholics about marriage. Some of what they have had to say is valuable, even at times helpful in a practical way. When their advice rings false, it is frequently discounted by married people on the grounds that the speaker, not having experienced marriage, couldn't really be expected to be authoritative. (This has been especially true in the area of sex. Couples whose marriages are at all decent know that sexual intercourse is a good deal more than a reproductive necessity, and in a happy marriage it is never primarily that. It is similarly not just a remedy for concupiscence, as some old manuals of moral theology had it. In fact, nothing seems to remedy concupiscence. If anyone has a cure short of Origen's—he was said to have castrated himself in a literal interpretation of the passage about making oneself a eunuch for the sake of the kingdom—it would be kind to let the rest of us know.)

Priests have on occasion offered the argument that an impartial observer of marriage can sometimes be a more qualified commentator than someone intimately involved. So, perhaps, a married layman might have something of value to say about celibacy; his authority will be as much as (and as limited as) the authority of a celibate on marriage. I invite the celibate reader to discount whatever seems unauthoritative or not quite to the point.

It may seem odd to discuss celibacy in a book which deals with marriage and other directly sexual things; but it makes sense for a couple of reasons. One is that in the Catholic tradition celibacy has often been seen as a holier choice, a higher state, than marriage. This is, I think, a misunderstanding, one which can lead us to focus our attention too much on the state of life itself and not on its meaning for the church as a whole. People marry or choose celibacy for any number of reasons, some simple, some complicated, not all of them generous, and those reasons can change over the course of a married or celibate life. The lives of some married people exhibit a grace the lives of some celibates do not, and vice-versa. And in any case it is wrong, in a tradition which invites us to choose the lower place, to speak of one calling as higher than another. A consideration of celibacy can throw some light on marriage, and marriage can throw some light on celibacy. This mutual illumination is important in a culture which devalues both marriage and celibacy.

It has been pointed out by a number of writers that celibacy is under attack from the culture at large (though in recent years it has become a more respectable option, usually for people who are licking their wounds after failed marriages or sad affairs), and within the Catholic church the discussion of a married clergy has in some cases been confused with a call to abolish celibacy altogether. I should make it clear here that I regard celibacy as an important thing; where it is genuine it is a gift to the church. I am not concerned here with celibacy as a *sine qua non* for the priesthood, but with the vow itself.

There is something essential in the fact that celibacy is a vowed state, not simply a condition like being single by choice or by accident, and in this it is like marriage. This is important, because vows, in and out of marriage, are increasingly regarded as less than central. I don't mean to suggest that those who seek a dispensation from vows—those of the celibate religious or those of marriage—are to be condemned for doing so; in many cases a release from those vows is a necessary thing. But it should be clear that what they are being dispensed from is ideally a binding and (to use an unfashionable word) absolute thing.

The Latin roots of the word *vow* are found in the words *devoted* and *devotion*. The devoted person is the person of the vow. There may be perfectly good reasons for which an individual would look for dispensation from a vow; but the possibility of dispensation should not make a vow seem at the start to be optional, something to be backed away from when things don't come up to expectations. Half-devotion is a contradiction in terms. There must be a whole-heartedness about undertaking the vowed life in any state; and it is a whole-heartedness which will simply have to be willed at times, especially in those dark times when there is no apparent reason to go on.

Western culture in recent years has tended to regard the idea of the vow as an anachronism based upon unreasonable expectations. A culture which is increasingly geared towards self-fulfillment and present satisfaction is not likely to be very sensitive in the way it looks at any vow. Vowing is, in a way, always done in the dark. It is an act of faith and hope: faith that what the vow entails is possible, and hope that the resources to make it possible will be there. There is something profoundly unreasonable about a vow—unreasonable here meaning beyond reason, not irrational. Any healthy young man or woman who takes a vow of celibacy, believing that he or she knows everything the vow will involve, will be proved wrong. A couple who marry usually do not, at the time of their marriage, really know one another very well. (They may think they do, but in retrospect they will find out how wrong they were.) The young celibate, or the young husband or wife, should know enough about the life being undertaken to be willing to stake everything on the vow; but this is precisely where the darkness begins, because we really do not know everything that will be asked of us.

The obvious question is, why do it at all? If there is an alternative to risking everything, why take the risk?

The answer is, I think, that without the vow we are much less likely to be led into the fullness of our humanity, which is a divine fullness. We will remain only human.

A vow is a symbol. Like all symbols, it has the power to evoke more than a merely rational or calculated response. To give your word before God that you will accept a vowed life, with anything it might involve, is an act of profound trust, which—if the vow is lived truly—draws you out of yourself, and draws from you responsibilities and capabilities which you didn't know were there. To vow is to step into a larger life than the life you control and manipulate. Any part of the self which holds back poisons the vow, and makes living it that much more difficult. Vows have a diminished importance today because of the individualism which pervades Western culture: unless something can be shown to be of obvious and more or less immediate benefit to the individual, its value is questioned. The vow challenges this mentality by suggesting that self-fulfillment and personal freedom, as good as they are, are not only not enough to make for a good life; a life which sets them as goals is too small a life. As

Christians we are called to something larger and stranger than the life the world offers us. We are called to a deeper life, which discloses itself during the course of our days and is fulfilled at death. This, anyway, is our hope, the risk we take, and our evidence (such as it is) that it makes sense to take this risk is to be found in the lives of people who went before us and lived well.

But if a vow, whether of marriage or of celibacy, calls us out of ourselves to a larger life—a participation in God's own life—what, specifically, does the vow of celibacy tell us about that life? Marriage is easier to understand, certainly. The desires for companionship, love-making, and children are universal and need no explanation. Within marriage there is the possibility of a knowing and a being known which is so archetypical of the soul's relationship to God that it is a recurrent theme in mystical literature (and of course, just as in the life of prayer, the knowing and being known involved in marriage can be humiliating and uncomfortable). Paul compares the love of one spouse for another to the love of Christ for the church. In marriage the natural and the supernatural meet wonderfully.

But celibacy? That's the strange one. There is not much in the Judaism from which Christianity sprang to make room for it. The nearly monastic Essene community (which may have had an influence on early Christianity) included celibates; but this was never common or encouraged in Judaism. The religions outside of Christianity which maintain celibate traditions tend either to deny or undervalue the goodness of the world. Yet in our tradition, which says firmly that the world is good, that sex and procreation are good, that pleasure well-taken is loved by God, there is this bunch of men and women who do not marry, who are pledged to a life of abstinence from sex.

There is nothing obviously good or healthy about celibacy. That alone should be looked at, because we live in an in-between time. We are close enough to a Christian culture, in which celibacy was generally accepted, to be blinded to its strangeness; and at the same time we are distant from any common understanding which could allow celibacy to be seen as the shocking and necessary thing it is. The development of this understanding matters as much as anything, if we are to see celibacy clearly. Consider this: celibacy seen as *desirable* would be neurotic, or selfish, or both. A person who refrains from marriage because he or she is afraid of the intimacy involved in marriage, or can't be bothered with it, or who does not want to be saddled with children, has made an ungenerous choice, a choice to be less than fully human. This is not at all what celibacy should be like.

Celibacy has been a part of Christian tradition from its beginning, but it was not demanded of all followers of Christ (except by some gnostics). But how does celibacy serve the Kingdom of God? If, as

Jewish and Christian tradition insists, creation is good, what is good or holy about renouncing the goodness of marriage and parenthood? The radical nature of celibacy demands the renunciation of something wholly good—a fact which presents us with a paradox.

Most explanations of celibacy try, one way or another, to resolve this paradox. There is, for example, the argument that the celibate is more available, more able to give himself to those in need, because he is not tied down to wife and child; in this way he is devoted wholly to the Kingdom in a way that married people cannot be.

I don't find this convincing. For one thing, I have yet to meet a celibate whose celibacy had directly to do with his availability. By this I do not mean that I have not met genuinely generous celibates—I have. But they were not *more* generous than the generous doctors I have known, or the generous married couples whose homes have been havens for many people, whose lives are open to those in need at every moment. And while there are types of work in which celibacy is, in a practical sense, more convenient (for example, the constant work of Mother Teresa and her sisters with Calcutta's dying, or the work of many others with the poor), even this kind of work has been done selflessly by married couples. An argument which puts practicality foremost, it seems to me, sells celibacy short.

Another argument is that the celibate, in committing his love to no particular person, is free to love everyone. But this contradicts the experience of love by making it a rationed thing, as if having spent 75 litres of love on one's wife and children, one had only 25 litres of God's allotment left for the rest of the race. In fact, by learning to love one other person deeply, one learns to love every other person that much more deeply. The love that men and women have for one another and for their children is, if it is Christian, carried into the rest of their lives and into every other relationship. Unless a person is capable of loving one other person deeply—and this is as true of celibates as it is of married people—he is not capable of loving *anyone*, much less everyone. There is nothing at all abstract about love; the Incarnation should teach us that much. And John reminds us that if we cannot love the one we see before us, we cannot love God, who cannot be seen.

Still another and more recent argument is that the celibate combines in himself both male and female elements, exhibiting a wholeness which others must seek in the opposite sex. But this also falls short of experience. In a good marriage a man and woman learn from one another's differences. "Masculine" and "feminine" attributes (which are increasingly seen as stereotypical, when they are gendered that way) must come together in any mature individual, celibate or married.

The paradoxical nature of celibacy should not be

explained away or made to look like a practical and beneficial thing. I believe it was Cardinal Suhard who said that as Christians we should live in such a way that, if God did not exist, our lives would make no sense. He did not mean that we are meant to put on a sort of show for the sake of the world, but rather meant to point out the risk of true Christianity: finally, you have to put everything on the line. It is unfortunate that asceticism has come to have such a bad name in recent years. Perhaps this bad name is the inevitable reaction to the misrepresentation of asceticism to which so many of us were exposed. Asceticism was made to look like a simple hatred or distrust of the flesh. This is unfortunate, because only within the context of a refreshed sense of the ascetic can celibacy make sense.

Celibacy is a kind of fast. Like fasting from food and drink, like voluntary poverty, it makes no worldly sense. Like fasting and voluntary poverty, celibacy is a witness to a life which is more profoundly real than the life offered by the world. Celibacy has no worldly justification (and this is why practical, sensible arguments in its favor sell it short, just as the argument that fasting is good for the figure misses the point of fasting), but it makes sense in the context of the reality of God's kingdom. Like fasting, it is a focussed thing: there is something about the life we are offered by God which demands a radical response, and celibacy is one way of responding radically. Like voluntary poverty, it may have to be a life-long commitment to bear the fruit it is meant to bear.

How are any of these things helpful? Fasting, like celibacy, means refraining from something good. It is a way of affirming that God alone is enough, is in fact everything we need, and it helps to focus our attention on God. During a fast we are reminded continuously (if sometimes uncomfortably) of what our lives are really about. The person who lives in radical simplicity, giving away what he does not need, has in a similar way put his life on the line.

Celibacy is in the same way a witness to the whole-heartedness the Gospel demands. This singleness must be present in every Christian life, not just the life of the celibate, but celibacy helps to illuminate it and throw it into relief. It is easy to say, for example, that I am ready to drop everything for the sake of the Kingdom, that once my hand is on the plow I will not turn back. It is willingness that matters, of course, but never to see that willingness tested can lead us into self-deception, and this is a lesson that fasting can begin to teach. At the level of the community, celibacy offers the same sort of witness to the married Christian. It is a manifestation of the fact that there is a love which suffices absolutely, and it is offered to each single human being, as well as to the community.

This love is what celibacy reveals, or should reveal. It is obviously not an easy witness to bear, and it is certainly not for everyone. It is a negative thing, in that it means self-denial, and at times whatever good it may offer will be invisible to the person who endures the loneliness which is an inevitable part of celibacy, for anyone with enough heart to love. The person who fasts from food will be hungry, and the person who fasts from sex, and the long intimate companionship of marriage, and from parenthood, will experience intense loneliness. Just as marriage and parenthood have their dark moments (there is no distance so lonely as the distance which can occur between two people who love one another, and a child's serious illness involves parents in an agony with which others may sympathize, but which can be truly shared only by someone who has gone through the same agony) so celibacy has a depth of loneliness which must be acknowledged—not to get it out of the way (that can't be done)—but to bring it to healing, by allowing the community to share as much of the burden as can be shared, and by asking the community to be available during the darkest moments.

One of the dangers of celibacy is the myth of self-sufficiency. The celibates I know who live it well are, not at all coincidentally, the ones who are capable of forming deep friendships, and who never give the sense of having erected protective emotional barriers. Many of them are members of religious orders, who come from communities human enough to provide their members with the mutual support and companionship which all of us must receive from our families and friends. I point this out because of the chilling barrenness which is too often encountered in rectories and convents, and in individual celibates whose inability to deal with the simplest heartfelt emotion is pitiful. A sour celibacy is as scandalous and hurtful to the community as a bad marriage.

In the Eastern churches it has been the typical practice to ordain married men, leaving celibacy to monks, from whom the bishops are chosen. This ancient discipline points up two things which the Western church sometimes obscures. One is that celibacy, like the monastic life, is a radical choice. The other is that it must be situated in an ascetic, contemplative context. Celibacy without asceticism and prayerfulness could become the most refined, subtle selfishness in the world. Perhaps Catholicism in the past did overemphasize the cross, suffering, and self-denial. But excluding these Christian facts is not the remedy; it is rather a surrender to the cultural surroundings that will allow only the sort of religion that fits in, the religion which reinforces the picture the world wants to have of itself. C.S. Lewis once remarked that there is always a tendency to warn an age against the danger into which it is least likely to fall; so in a puritanical age we are warned against licentiousness, and in a licentious age we are warned against puritanism. It isn't the dangers of asceticism that the Western world needs to fear right now.

There is one final, pastoral aspect of celibacy which I would like to mention. There are people who remain unmarried and unloved because they have not been able, for whatever reasons, to attract anyone. In looking at a married person someone in this situation is able to say, "That person lives in such security, the security of being loved—he couldn't possibly understand my loneliness." The fact that the other person is loved stands as a barrier between them. The celibate can reveal to someone this lonely a love which can be healing, and can restore a meaning and dignity which the world denies.

Celibacy seen only as a "state in life" is as cold as ice, just as dead as a marriage which exists only as a pledge on paper. It must exhibit the love it is based in, the paradoxical strength in weakness of which Paul boasts, or it will be worthless.

A NOTE ON MARRIAGE
AND FRIENDSHIP

ONE night a seminarian friend told me that he was leaving the seminary. His reason was that he had become very close to another seminarian—their friendship meant so much to him and was so extraordinarily profound that he was sure marriage would be an even deeper thing, and he did not want to take a vow which might prevent him from marrying. I was pleased that his friendship was that rare and good sort, but I was not at ease with his assumption about marriage. I am not sure that marriage and friendship are on the same continuum, although they are certainly related. A marriage without friendship would be (and too often is) a living hell.

But there is a difference. Some months ago I read an article that bothered me, and bothered me enough to force an articulation of what that difference is. The article told of a priest who in the course of counseling a women parshioner fell in love. He and his lover (she became that) felt unjustly bound by the vows he had taken. The article implied that there was something essentially wrong with a permanent vow of celibacy because of the agony this couple were put through.

What bothered me was not that people do feel this way—perhaps he should have sought laicization, and it might indeed have been a good thing for them to marry. But what I wondered was how his situation differed from that of a man who has taken a vow of marriage, who meets a woman after he is married and falls deeply in love with her.

One answer, the best one, is that a vow of celibacy does not involve a specific other person the way a vow of marriage does. (To say that the other person involved is God is not quite right; God is as much involved in the vow of marriage.) Another answer, an increasingly popular one, is that the two situations don't differ at all, basically, and it makes sense for the man who has fallen in love with another woman to leave his wife for her. But for those of us to take marriage seriously this isn't the right answer.

In fact it is possible for married men and women to be attracted—sometimes attracted strongly—by other men and women after they have vowed fidelity to one other person for the rest of their lives. That ought to be made clear to young people before they marry (older people will already have found it out), so that the experience of infatuation after marriage isn't profoundly unsettling to them. When something of this sort happens it should not be seen as destructive to the marriage, or as something which calls the marriage commitment into doubt. It is a normally healthy, human response to another person's attractiveness; there is even a sense in which it would be a lack of appreciation *not* to respond this way. But it does wound a marriage, sometimes fatally, when infatuation leads to infidelity. The vow must be kept for the sake of the wholeness of the marriage. And if it is kept, infatuation can turn into friendship. In the long run, this sort of friendship is a deeper and longer-lasting thing than infatuation is.

A vow—whether of marriage or of celibacy—can free us for friendship. And this is where friendship and marriage differ. The vow paradoxically binds us in order to free us, and what it frees us for is friendship. Without the vow we would be back in the adolescent world of sexual game-playing; and where vows are not taken seriously we are back there.

I tried to convince my seminarian friend that he would not experience a deeper closeness in marriage than in friendship, but another kind of depth and another kind of closeness. Both friendship and marriage require loyalty, toleration, an acceptance of the other's weaknesses as well as an appreciation of the other's strengths and virtues, forgiveness, companionship, and at times extreme self-sacrifice. Marriage and friendship can be so profoundly satisfying as to make you rejoice and give praise and thanksgiving.

But they work on different levels. Marriage requires a vow, for all sorts of reasons. One of them involves the permanence necessary for the creation of a home. The other involves the importance of sexual fidelity. Fidelity in marriage has to involve more than sexual fidelity; but it has to involve at least that—to allow sexual infatuation to deepen into sexual friendship in marriage, and to free us for friendship with all of the attractive people who live outside our marriage vows.

PART TWO

Disputed Questions

CATHOLICS AND SEX

NOT too long ago the national news held up for all to see the case of a man and woman in the Catholic diocese of Joliet, Illinois. They were refused permission to marry in the Catholic church on the grounds that the man was impotent as a result of a spinal injury. Because he could not have a normal sexual relationship with his wife he couldn't have a wife at all, according to the priest who refused them permission to marry. Here a law which ought to have been a protection for the wife (you marry someone, and find out after the ceremony that he's impotent; you should have a way out) was turned against a couple who knew the score in advance and still wanted to be together. A very short time thereafter the bishop of the diocese said that the couple could marry after all, but not before the country had been offered an embarrassing look at the legalism which poisons too many Catholic approaches to sex and marriage.

In many respects the picture of Catholicism as a uniquely awful school of sexual guilt is a caricature. Once, by coincidence, I ran across references to Catholic guilt, Jewish guilt, and Protestant guilt during a three-day period. Catholics really don't have a monopoly on the phenomenon. And guilt has its uses: there are times when I ought to feel guilty, because I've behaved badly. Guilt, when it isn't the morbid and never-ending sort, is the heart's way of telling you not to behave badly again.

A strictly therapeutic, value-free approach to sex is one extreme, but the way a lot of us were taught is another. The sixth and ninth commandments were the only two which didn't seem to have any venial sins attached to them—everything in this area, unlike the areas of charity, justice to the poor, or honesty, was fraught with eternal peril. Sex had less to do with love and commitment (not to speak of mutual pleasure) than with picking your way across a minefield of possible mortal sins. While there was some talk of sex as beautiful and holy it was pretty ethereal. At the practical level there were manuals of moral theology which insisted that unless a sexual act could lead to impregnation it was illicit, and which said that a woman had a duty to submit sexually to a drunken or abusive husband. (I know: the same book would have said that it was wrong for the husband to be abusive and drunk. There is still something ugly here.)

Something as old as Catholicism cannot be judged solely by the standards of the most recent thought and cultural prejudice, and this is too frequently what is done when Catholicism's allegedly negative views of sexuality are discussed. But it is also important not to exempt even an ancient tradition from responsibility for its bad ideas and bad effects, and sex is one area in which at least one approach to Catholicism—the Jansenist variety which had a powerful presence in American Catholic schools —can fairly be said to have done damage to people. If other traditions have done the same sort of damage, that should not be an occasion for Catholic self-congratulation or self-absolution. Christianity claims to deal with incarnation, with the belief that God so loves humanity that he became human to show us the depths of divine solidarity, taking on the fullness of everything flesh means, a fullness filled with divine life, to show us the extent to which love can go. Nothing human is alien to a love like that. It could be argued that Christianity, of all religions, ought to be the one which deals more sensitively with sex than any other, or at least as sensitively as any, given the importance flesh plays in its claims.

But at the moment the church's teaching about sex is in disarray. There are liberal and conservative factions whose positions are so far apart as to appear irreconcilable, each accusing the other of being either unorthodox and unfaithful to the *magisterium*, or inhumane and legalistic.

There is little dialogue across the gulf between these positions. Each side overstates its case, and fails to acknowledge its own weaknesses, while refusing to hear the concerns behind the other side's rhetoric. This failing is not limited to disputes about sexuality; it is general. The thing no one ever wants to admit is that about some subjects we may not really know very much. We are terrified of saying that there are some vitally important questions about which we have no compelling answers, only a few stray clues and some general guidelines—enough, perhaps, to get us through life in a ragged sort of way, but nothing so compelling that we can say much with total assurance.

Not knowing scares the hell out of us. The principle that in certain things there should be unity, in doubtful things liberty, and in all things charity is an ancient Catholic sentiment. It has too often remained merely a sentiment and has not been honored enough, because no one who was passionate about any subject was prepared to admit that there was anything doubtful about it at all.

Perhaps it is because sex is so intimate a subject, so close to the centers of our lives, whether we are married, single, heterosexual or homosexual, that it has inspired the passionate defense of more half-formed ideas than any other subject in Catholic history, and unlike specific doctrinal debates (whether usury ought to be allowed, for example, or how to reconcile Donatist heretics to the church) it won't go away as long as we keep on being born into bodies with genitals and psyches with sexual urges as strong as the moon's pull at the ocean's tides.

Until it crumbles, the conservative case often seems to be the stronger because it appears to have the weight of history behind it. Our forefathers felt the way I do, the conservative says when faced with a fresh or an upstart idea—what do *you* have to offer that's better? And there is general good advice in the old caution that no one should abandon the folkways without reason. The conservative attitude which asks a new idea to explain itself is a wise one: what good reasons do you have to offer for striking a new course, or for abandoning an old one?

The problem is that having asked that wise question the conservative tends to wrap himself defensively around the folkways, refusing to listen to the answer, or looking—before the words are out of his opponent's mouth—for the flaw in his logic. The idea that there could be anything wrong or even limited about the ideas to which you cling is terribly difficult to accept, particularly where something as intimately connected to you as sex is involved, and the usual solution is not to accept the possibility at all.

On the other side, the problem is that it is easy to find current ideas more compelling than older ones. The current ideas come to us looking and feeling fresh; in the older ones we smell old dentures and hear the echos of grade school corridors. The older ideas are lit with the dim auras of parental disapproval and consequent negative personal feelings. How much better to accept this newly-minted idea, which not only comes to us free of those associations but has its own logic, which helps us see old problems in a new light, without negative associations

which can cloud our perceptions and confuse issues
about which we need some clarity. The trouble with
this is that some presuppositions are so much a part
of the zeitgeist that they are transparent to us; we are
unaware of them because they seem simply true.
They are such pervasive ingredients in a commonly
accepted worldview that they seem as certainly and
unquestionably true as the worldview of medieval
people or renaissance people seemed to them. But
in fact these presuppositions are as historically condi-
tioned and limited as the ideas which we are temp-
ted to reject.

The problem with the conservative position is that
it seems right because it is old. But there have been
many contradictory conceptions of vitally important
subjects which were defended on the same grounds,
and tradition has defended bad as well as good
causes. The problem with the liberal vision is that it
tends not to see the historical limitation of its own
perception.

There is no single Christian attitude towards sex.
Early Christians, because they were Jews, accepted
the prevailing Jewish attitudes towards sex,
illuminated by what the revelation of Christ showed
them, and it led to some apparent contradictions: on
the one hand Paul can say that in Christ there is
neither male nor female; on the other he says that
women can't prophesy or have their heads un-
covered during the liturgy. As Christianity became
one of the many religious voices heard in the

Hellenic culture of the Empire, and was forced to speak the common philosophical language of that culture, it adopted many of the Hellenic attitudes towards sex and women, attitudes which were on the whole more negative than those of the Judaism from which Christianity sprang. Contacts with the tribes which were Christianized during Christianity's move into the West forced the incorporation of tribal attitudes into the Christian understanding of marriage. There was a time when the dowry was considered as essential a part of marriage as the consent of the people involved; economically (and this was no small part of the consideration) it was more important. At various times the fact of consent, agreement between the families involved, and the sexual consummation of marriage have been seen as the necessary ingredients of a valid marriage.

The attitudes which have influenced Catholic Christianity's understanding of sexuality range from Judaism to Stoic and Platonic philosophy, Augustine's rather gloomy outlook, the influence of monasticism, and the reaction to a number of heresies—all of these elements bearing their share of wisdom, but also trailing some shadows as well, as anything hobbled by being enfleshed will. Anything incarnate is given at once to life and death, and contains life-giving and deathly elements. It is impossible to know from within one's own sense of these things that any particular attitude is completely healthy and untainted by any negative element. (Even the category of "healthy" and "healthy-minded" is peculiarly Victorian and limited.)

It is important to know two things at once, especially in a time when thinking about sexuality tends towards polemical attitudes. One is that all attitudes towards sexuality were formed by the times in which the people who had them happened to live. There is no one golden age in which people thought clearly and wonderfully about sexuality. The other is that our own age, with its own set of prejudices, is as limited as any other and as unlikely—and at the same time and for the same reason just as likely—to offer us the insights we need to judge these things intelligently. The insights of medievel mystics may tell us more about marriage than any modern marriage manual. At the same time, our age is likely more than any other to tell us things we need to know about early childhood experiences and their relationship to our later emotional and sexual makeup.

One thing seems certain about the contemporary Catholic scene: *Humanae Vitae* brought an end to the time in which people looked for all of the rules to be spelled out in detail. Catholics who had tried for years to follow church teaching in matters relating to sex and marriage decided not to bother. The reason may be that after Vatican II there was a dawning sense that the laity were not merely clients of the clergy but were the church, every bit as much as those ordained to administer the sacraments. There are other reasons, though, and they have to do with the encyclical itself, and the context in which it was issued.

Although *Humanae Vitae* is considered a dead issue by many, because everyone seems to have come to an unshakeable opinion about its absolute ban on artificial contraception, its arguments and their widespread rejection remain important. The encyclical's real insights were easily ignored, because so much emphasis was given to the rejection of artifical contraception.

The context in which *Humanae Vitae* was issued made its acceptance unlikely. When the rhythm method was declared to be an acceptable way to limit family size, a contraceptive intention was also accepted. The argument against the rhythm method had been that these things ought to be left to providence; now it was considered all right to limit the size of your family, so long as the technique was an aceptable one. The hope of people who practice natural family planning is that this particular sexual act, while it might in some technical sense be "open to the transmission of life," won't *really* be. Their hearts are where the hearts of those using artifical contraception are; it is their method that is different. Now technique, not intention, became the debating point. Hydraulics rather than the heart was the focus of moral concern. And there were other questions: isn't time in its way a physical thing? It is argued that the use of natural family planning demands restraint and self-sacrifice; but it has to be demonstrated that there is a good reason to prefer a less effective means of preventing conception to a more effective one, because the unstated assumption behind this argument is that it is better to do without sex on a periodic basis than it is to make love, and, given the contraceptive intention of both rhythm and artificial contraception, it has to be shown why this ought to be preferred. In any good marriage restraint and self-denial will show up often enough without having to build them into the system.

In the years before *Humanae Vitae* there was a widespread feeling that the church was headed towards change on this issue, and indeed it was, though the change which happened was not quite what anyone anticipated then. The Vatican itself was plainly affected by this feeling, and encouraged it with the formation of a papal commission which looked into the issue. The fact that a commission was asked to do this was understood by many as a clear indication that contraception was an open question. The commission recommended changes in the traditional teaching. Its recommendations were ignored, *Humanae Vitae* was issued, and in its turn it, too, was ignored. Pope Paul said that the church was not in doubt, but that part of the church most intimately involved in the sacrament of marriage plainly did not accept his reading of the mind of the church.

This was a radical change. For one thing, the authority of the hierarchy to speak in a binding way in the area of sex and marriage was quietly rejected by most married couples, without an apparent crisis of faith. Some eighty percent of married Catholic couples of childbearing age who regularly go to communion also use some form of artificial contraception. The decline in confessions makes it clear that they do not regard this as a matter which requires absolution. The radical nature of this rejection has implications which go beyond the question of marriage: if the heirarchy aren't authoritative here, are they in other matters? Can what they say in any area be accepted without question? Should it ever have been? This sort of probing used to be the preserve of Catholic intellectuals; it was not, before *Humanae Vitae,* common at the parish level. No one denies the need for the hierarchy, but their place in the church is clearly not what it was from the time of the counter-reformation until Vatican II, and it won't go back to being what it was. This may be deplored by those for whom the hierarchy's unquestionable authority represented security, or it may be celebrated by those who believe that the hierarchy's function involves a more profound listening than the history of *Humanae Vitae* reveals, but it is a fact of life however one feels about it.

And it has created a vacuum. The old form of authority can't fill it; there is no new form of authority or question-answering which can. The problem is not the confusion of people who would be set straight by clear and unambiguous answers, as some conservatives argue; people who want clear and unambiguous answers will always be able to find them. The problem is that there are important questions which have pastoral implications, and they are not being dealt with well. Some of them involve sex.

If the acceptance of the rhythm method was the camel's nose under the tent, a whole caravan began to force its way in after the first camel. If rhythm, with its use of that physical thing, time, was a permissible way to limit family size, why not other means of arriving at the same result? Natural law got stretched very thin in some of these arguments. (Karl Barth wrote to Paul VI to suggest that one problem with *Humanae Vitae* was that it raised natural law to the level of revelation.) But the problem goes deeper than that: if the rhythm method was allowed because it allowed people to limit their family's size, the other side of that coin is the acknowledgement that sex is a good thing, or at the very least not a bad thing, quite apart from its reproductive possibilities. This is hardly news, and it has been celebrated in the wider Catholic culture for years, but its official acknowledgement opened all sorts of problems with traditional Catholic approaches to some difficult sexual questions. One of them involves homosexuality. Catholic moral theology never said that it was wrong to be homosexual—in this it was more humane than fundamentalism. Since homosexuality, like heterosexuality, is not primarily a matter of choice, the simple fact of being homosexual cannot be considered a moral problem. But moral theologians did maintain that homosexual acts—like the acts of heterosexuals which are not "open to the transmission of life"—are sinful, and more or less for the same reason: because they cannot be procreative and are therefore unnatural. I know of at least one moral theologian who has rejected contraception on the grounds that its logic leads to the possibility that homosexuality may not require celibacy. It could be argued that our current state of knowledge, or lack of knowledge, ought to require some humility here, and an acknowledgement that there is a lot we simply do not know.

Still, despite our lack of knowledge, despite the contradictions which can be found in our tradition, there are things which need to be said. There are people whose implicit argument is that sex is the single area in which there can be no prohibitions, the one area of life in which absolutely anything done between consenting adults is OK. A definitely vile bunch has floated the argument that children are fair game for adult sexual services. The problem is that consenting adults can agree to defraud, deceive, rob, mug, or torment others; an agreement between a slaver and a potential slave would not change the basic fact that slavery demeans the slave owner and the slave both. Sexuality, however private a thing it may be, has a social resonance and leads to social obligations which go beyond the tiny circle drawn around two consenting adults to include a wider set of relationships.

Despite its legalism, *Humanae Vitae* said some

things about the contraceptive mentality which very much needed to be said. For one thing, it condemned the belief that one must always be in control of one's life; the scientistic notion that we are most human when we are absolutely in control was pointed out as a danger. The emphasis on natural family planning is an attempt to keep us from severing our link to a world we are part of, not simply in charge of. The separation of sex from reproduction has not been an unmixed blessing; it has led, to give one example, to a belief that pregnancy must either be a matter of deliberate choice, or of contraceptive failure. This implies that life, to be of value, depends primarily upon our choice, our welcoming. The life that happens "by accident" or "despite precautions" is felt to be less valuable. This is not a healthy or decent attitude. Nor is the attitude which regards any suffering, inconvenience, or call to sacrifice as an evil to be got rid of. *Humanae Vitae* addressed those questions, but because its legalistic conclusions didn't square with the experience of the people to whom it was addressed it was dismissed. Its genuine insights deserve rescuing and an evangelistic, rather than legalistic, presentation.

The problem with legalism here is that it does not address the whole of a human situation. While there are certainly problems with the contraceptive mentality, important ones, an anti-contraceptive mentality carries its own set of problems as well. While it makes more room for the unexpected, and calls on people to make sacrifices, the sacrifices are sometimes much too severe and would not be considered blessed in another context. The obituaries of the nineteenth century are full of women who died in childbirth, and of men who died after having been married three or four times, fathering several children by each wife. Childbearing led to the death of many of those women. There are problems with the contraceptive mentality. There are at least as many with the mentality that finds contraception simply an evil.

In trying to see these questions clearly we have to admit, first of all, that we can't. No one is objective about sex. For too many years celibates told non-celibates what they ought to be about, sexually, without listening much to the people whose experience included years of lovemaking. A sex-obsessed age assumes that celibates must be neurotic or undersexed, and celibates are seen as people who could not possibly have chosen their way of life freely and for non-neurotic reasons; this is also absurd. Heterosexuals assume that homosexuals are sick; but that would be impossible to know, since if homosexuality were simply the sexual equivalent of left-handedness, as some have suggested, we would have to be able to see it without the layers of prejudice with which our culture has surrounded it. (Is a monogamous homosexual sicker than a heterosexual Don Juan? Is anyone completely healthy here?)

Nobody is very clear about this mysterious and fascinating mess. We talk a lot about needs when what we mean is powerful wants; people break up marriages on that ground. Our age is clearly weird where sex is concerned; so was Augustine's. We have to remember that after more than a million years of evolution, including the evolution of everything we cover under the heading of human sexuality, the human race has had only a comparatively few thousand years of the sort of culture which asks questions about itself. During that time we have produced Buddhist monastic writings which say that monks who have erotic dreams and nocturnal emissions have failed in their discipline, Jewish proscriptions against making love to menstruating women, Biblical fundamentalists who insist that a man must be his wife's master, and Catholic manuals of moral theology which say that masturbation is mortally sinful. A lot of what we regard as Christian doctrine on this subject comes from Greek philosophy, which was at odds with the Jewish acceptance of the flesh as good.

People who want clear behavioral guidelines are in for a bad time these days. I haven't been inside a Catholic high school for years, but I wouldn't be surprised if fewer Catholic adolescents ask their teachers how far they can go before they commit a mortal sin. Aside from such obvious things as the condemnation of adultery and a general rejection of divorce, the New Testament has very little to say about sex, which is probably just as well. Our guidelines include loving our neighbor as we love ourselves, and forgiving one another as we have been forgiven. That plays hell with people who want to be legalistic about matters which have to do, finally, with compassion and tenderness. If there is any rule about sex it must involve these things, and unselfishness, and fidelity to the commitments you've made, as well as an awareness of the possibility of self-deception, which is the easiest thing in the world to fall into. Beyond that, I really don't know. I don't think anybody does.

ABORTION

MOST of us are tired of the issue of abortion. Just about everything wrong with both sides of the issue has been discussed by now, including the inconsistencies that mark both sides—for example, there are hawkish, pro-death penalty right-to-lifers, and there are pro-choice people who care more about the survival of baby harp seals than about unborn human beings.

There are exceptions on both sides: Magda Denes and Linda Bird Francke have both written books which deal with the difficulty of abortion from a pro-choice perspective. Although I disagree with many of their conclusions, I can find some common ground with people who see that the issue has tragic dimensions, and involves decisions about life, and the taking of life. There are pro-life people who see the connection between abortion, the patterns of social oppression that make abortion seem desirable, and the anti-human direction of the arms race.

Between the reasonable parties on both sides (and there are not many of them) the discussion is much like the debate over the just war theory: some believe that war, tragic as it is, is justifiable under certain circumstances; others believe that the justification of war is itself one of war's causes. Both at least agree that war is a tragic thing. To dismiss the element of tragedy involved in any decision to take life (as many defenders of abortion do) or to dismiss the inconsistencies which are involved in the argument that pre-natal life is sacred, but the life of a criminal or an enemy is not, is to avoid the real point at issue.

But despite our weariness, despite the degenerating argument, the issue won't go away. It is about something too important, and the significance of the issue extends beyond the specific problem of abortion.

Pluralism has hit a real obstacle here. Law has confused the issue profoundly, but that is to be expected in a democracy, where law becomes the common ground of argument. The problem is that by a kind of idolatrous leap law becomes not only the common ground (since we accept no other common authority) but the source of all judgment, the only standard, as if law's function were not to reflect justice but to create it. Discussions about abortion frequently lead to the question, "Should people be *allowed*, or *forbidden*, to have abortions?" The implication, too often, is that what is forbidden for legal reasons is bad, and what is allowed is good, and the overlap between law and justice happens so neatly, with such thorough congruence, that the question becomes a matter of what can or should be imposed upon people by the state. Law and morality embrace, wisdom is equated with legislation, and Caesar is lord over all.

Everyone is let off the hook this way. No one needs to persuade anyone of the truth, the wisdom, or the decency of a particular position. But surely this is what must be done where the issue is as important as abortion, and the country is so nearly evenly divided. Where law is made the absolute standard the issue itself becomes less important than the desire to win, to force an interpretation not only of law but of life on someone else.

Pro-choice people often accuse pro-life people of doing just that. In their view reasonableness requires an open-ended view of human life and its origins, one which in the absence of clear and agreed-upon definitions of humanity would allow abortion to those who choose it. It cannot be proven that fetal life is human; therefore it may be taken. But to accept this as the proper view of tolerance in a democracy is to accept a particular orthodoxy. To insist that in the absence of a proof of human life, human life may be taken, is to make a moral judgment as arbitrary as any made by the right-to-life people. The assumption here is that the value of human life depends absolutely on our definition of human life. If we cannot agree on a definition, then we must allow any liberty at all to be taken with the subject under discussion—whether that subject is unborn, retarded, or comatose. Those three conditions, after all, do play rough with definitions of humanity which require us to put at the center of our defining such qualities as consciousness, self-awareness, and the ability to form meaningful relationships.

The ordinary pro-choice argument assumes that there is no intrinsic value to life. Value is given, or withheld, by human beings. It is not a quality which is inherent in the fact of our having been conceived.

No one, for example, argues that life in some form does not begin with conception. Everyone agrees that unless it is interfered with, what begins at conception will become what we call human. What is argued about is whether life at that point matters. Mystery is a bad word these days, but mystery and reverence are involved here. There is, in the argument that we may kill a life which cannot be proven human, a total lack of any sense of human mystery, a lack of love for the darkness all of us come from. To fail to regard it with love or reverence, to see it as a possible killing ground, is a sign of what we think of humanity.

This is a religious issue, as slavery was, as war always is, as the arms race is and will be. It isn't the religion most Americans are comfortable with, the publicly acceptable variety which endorses the way we live. It is religious insofar as it involves attitudes towards life and life's meaning which lie beyond the realm of proof and disproof. What is not commonly seen is that it is religious on both sides: the people who oppose the anti-abortion movement on what they consider reasonable democratic grounds are, more often than not, believers in a worldview as undemonstrable as that of their opponents. The pro-life people believe that life's value is inherent in the fact of its being there at all. They believe that life is given. Given-ness implies a giver, and a value conferred in the simple fact of existence. That is, plainly, religious. But to argue that life has no inherent value, or to argue that if there is such a value it matters so little that we may agree to disagree and stand by while lives whose value cannot be proven are destroyed—this is to argue something equally metaphysical, equally undemonstrable. Such an argument says that value is conferred only, or at least most importantly, by human beings. Many pro-choice people want a surrender to their worldview, which was born at the Enlightenment. Their resentment is that an older orthodoxy is not willing to accept their victory, and die quietly.

Some abortion proponents have argued that Catholic opposition to abortion is itself rather recent, and that the ancient idea of "ensoulment" was once interpreted as allowing abortion up until a certain point in the pregnancy. It is true that there was a distinction made between the time of conception and the later time of "quickening" or "ensoulment," at which time some theologians believed that the fetus received a human soul. This distinction—which was based in an inadequate understanding of physiology—was not, however, construed as permission to abort. Such an interpretation was explicitly ruled out, and the distinction between the time before and after ensoulment was dismissed by many theologians as beside the point, since what began at conception was in any case in the process of becoming human, and its life was therefore sacred.

Explicit papal condemnations of abortion are late, but so is an absoutely centralized and authoritarian papacy. Abortion was explicitly condemned in the first century *Didache,* in Tertullian, in Basil, in the *Epistle of Barnabas,* and in the response of a second-century convert who replied to the pagan charge that Christians were guilty of human sacrifice by asking, "How can we kill a man, when we are those who say that all who use abortifacients are homicides, and will account to God for their abortions as for the killing of men. For the fetus in the womb is not an animal." John Chrysostom said of men who encouraged their mistresses to abort that in doing so they encouraged them to be murderers as well as prostitutes. This opposition to abortion is the consistent Catholic teaching, and was made most pointed by Clement of Alexandria, who associated the destruction of the child in the womb with the loss of love for humanity. (The examples quoted here come, most of them, from John Noonan's essay "An Almost Absolute Value in History" in his *The Morality of Abortion* [Harvard, 1970]. One does not have to agree with all of Noonan's conclusions to find his history impressive, certainly more impressive than the thinking which finds in the ambiguity surrounding life's beginning a permission to take life.)

A society which can accept the killing of humanity at its most vulnerable stage is not compassionate. That seems safe enough to say. And of course our society is not; abortion isn't the only sign of our lack of compassion. So is the mentality which makes abortion seem desirable to women who are pregnant and fear the consequences. They are the victims of an uncompassionate, unhelpful society. A Catholic girl's school near me expels girls who get pregnant, and in doing so they surely contribute to a climate which makes abortion look like a solution to a difficult problem.

It is true that there is nothing new about abortion, and since ancient times infanticide was the common solution to the problem of unwanted children. (There are those who argue that abortion is more humane than infanticide, but I don't agree; many pro-choice arguments can be used to defend infanticide as well as abortion.) Abortion is not new, but the common acceptance of it as a decent option is relatively new. Abortion and infanticide were considered acceptable in ancient Rome. Infanticide was most commonly used then to get rid of female children. Jews and Christians were considered odd for their opposition to the use of abortifacients. But Rome—which saw so many of its people as property, to be used in whatever way the owner desired—is not a model we want to imitate, though there are those today who are just as callous as many Romans were. A child's sex can be determined early on now, and children have been aborted for having been unfortunate enough to be the wrong sex.

It has been argued that abortion is more merciful than bringing an unwanted child into a life of probable suffering. It is true that an unwanted child suffers. So does a wanted child, eventually; all of us suffer in some way, and all of us will die. If society or parents reject any human being who might suffer, or whose suffering might impose a burden on others, the problem is not with the victim but with the hardness of heart which the victim encounters. Old and retarded people are often not wanted, but I dread the thought that we might put into practice the idea that there is anything merciful or loving about making their lives easier by getting rid of them.

A friend of mine has cerebral palsy. She knows that if this condition could have been predicted she might have been aborted. She has suffered; it has not been easy for her to get through life. But her life has involved marriage, divorce, childbirth, motherhood, political and religious struggles, intellectual and moral growth, unhappiness, and joy. Someone with good intentions could have prevented all that. She is opposed to abortion; she does not regard her life as an unhappiness to be prevented. There are people who would have saved her from her life. It would have burdened them to witness her struggle; it might even have caused them pain. I find the triumph of her life infinitely more important than their interpretation of what her life should have been like to be worth living. I am glad that they were not able to impose their brand of mercy.

DIVORCE

MY first reaction when I hear of the divorce of people I know is often an irrational combination of irritation and fear. There is so much of it going on that you feel almost as if it might be catching, and some of the fear is personal: you look at all the holes in your own heart, all of the usually unacknowledged darkness, and sense the germs stirring there. And then the irritation: why *them*? They could have done things differently; it doesn't need to end up this way...and of course, it might not "need to," but there are points beyond which a marriage is not at all likely to survive.

It is frightening to see marriage after marriage crumbling. It is a fear not only for yourself but for a culture which some day will learn the result (it isn't likely to be a happy one) of so many families coming apart at the center, and the pain isn't one which can be cured completely by amicable agreements following the divorces (though they certainly are better than bitterness). A nun I know associated the phenomenon of priests and nuns leaving their own commitments with the phenomenon of divorce. She acknowledged the differences: specific people are hurt more deeply when a marriage ends, and that fact makes a profound difference, but her point was a cultural one. "I know some people who really should leave the priesthood and sisterhood, and there are people whose marriages should end—but not as many people as this!" A vow must make deep sense to feel binding, and our culture doesn't offer much support for the slow learning in the dark which is a part of many ancient and traditional cultures. Where immediate understanding and self-satisfaction are considered to be primary parts of a good life, the whole idea of vowing begins to be eclipsed.

But apart from this, the current instability is even a socially awkward thing. You call a friend you haven't seen for years and ask how he is; you're afraid to ask how his wife is because too many times you've been told, "We've split up." The pain caused to children is nearly enough to make you a believer in trial marriage: let people live together for awhile, make their mistakes, and after they've messed things up let them split before they have children. The problem with this is not only the obvious moral problem involved in people living together without any real commitment, but the unfortunate fact that people who have lived together for years and who decide to get married tend to split up as often as people who didn't live together before marriage.

There is no novitiate for marriage, and it is not at all apparent that any novitiate could be designed which would offer a guarantee—or even a reliable indication—that everything will go all right once the vows have been pledged. In most Catholic parishes and dioceses there are encouragements (and in some there are strict rules) which move engaged couples through courses of instruction and careful consideration before marriage is allowed. In a fair number of cases this has led some participants to a decision *not* to marry, and this is not at all a bad thing. But the other side of what looks like churchly coercion is that some couples are not willing to take orders from clerics, and they ignore the process and get married outside of the church. I found it interesting that a friend of mine who is no longer Catholic was more sympathetic towards the idea of a required pre-marital course of study than are many of the Catholics I know. But he has a personal stake in the problem: a couple of his brothers have gone through disastrous, painful divorces, and he is willing to see any method used to prevent that kind of suffering.

My own opinion is that a long engagement is extremely important. To hell with whirlwind courtships and romantic views of what your life might be like together; you ought to be together long enough to see the other at his or her worst, and you should spend time talking about everything from relationships with the inlaws to the religious upbringing of your children. The idea of a long engagement used to be discouraged—perhaps because some people took such unfair advantage of it (as in the old joke about the Irishman who, after many years, proposed to his fiancee by asking, "Would you like to be buried with my people?") but primarily, I'm afraid, because there was some worry that sexual temptation would get the better of the engaged couple. That risk matters so much less than the risks attending a disastrous marriage that it makes a long engagement more than worth it (and should this really ever have been a problem?) Learning who the other is takes time and reflection, and it is too important to make the mistake of rushing through the process.

Despite every precaution things still sometimes go disastrously wrong, and a marriage which once seemed right falls apart. The first lesson people who have made a marriage learn, once they have made that absurd life-long commitment, is how little they know one another—and for that matter, how little they know themselves. They are thrown bound and blindfolded right into the middle of a situation which is by definition absolutely new to them. What if the lessons aren't learned right—or if one person is trying to learn but the other isn't willing? Or what if some profound misunderstanding makes a continuing marriage impossible? While we are called to forgive again and again, there are some marriages in which it is best to do that forgiving at a distance; in some cases there are marriages which are physically and psychologically too dangerous to continue.

There is no doubt that from a scriptural point of view divorce is not a desireable thing, and Jesus' words suggest that except where adultery is involved (and even this passage is unclear) divorce is not permitted and remarriage is wrong.

Does this mean that the divorced person has gone through something meaningless from a Christian point of view, or that the divorced person is not a follower of Jesus, or cannot be a follower of Jesus? If that were the case it would be unique in the gospels.

Jesus was not, as some have suggested, a deliberate upsetter of the law, a man who tried to overturn Jewish tradition. In his attitude towards marriage he was most probably influenced by the two greatest Jewish teachers of his time, Hillel and Shammai. As noted earlier, Hillel was on the whole the more liberal. With regard to most issues regarding the law Jesus shows himself to be in line with Hillel's sort of thinking. A clear exception is in the matter of divorce. Hillel was notoriously easy where the grounds of divorce were concerned; Shammai was much stricter. Jesus went even beyond Shammai in his condemnation of divorce. Like any good Jew, Jesus reverenced the law, but he did not regard it in a fundamentalist way. With regard to marriage he went beyond the law. He was stricter, where divorce was concerned, than the law required him to be.

This is unusual, because in nearly every other way Jesus is revealed as part of the liberal school of rabbis. Even though he says the smallest part of the law must not be set aside, he says that "the sabbath was made for man; man was not made for the sabbath." He is not legalistic about marriage, but the latitude which is shown in some other areas—the observance of the sabbath, for instance—is not only not shown here; here he points to a standard more exacting than the most conservative interpretation of the law.

This is not necessarily a contradiction. If we see Jesus' attitude towards marriage as a contradiction of a normally liberal attitude towards the law, it means that we have made the mistake of seeing marriage as something which is supposed to be under the law. If instead we see Jesus' teaching on marriage as part of the spirit which he directs us towards in the sermon on the mount, the import of his teaching and marriage is put into its proper context. The sermon on the mount teaches us that the law is not so much wrong as it is completely inadequate; it does not touch the depths of what our relationship with God means.

It is not our place to judge those who have failed to live up to Jesus' "rules" about marriage. Those rules are not rules in any ordinary sense; they aren't laws. They are more like his statement that those who seek their lives will lose them, or his counsel to be perfect, as God is perfect. Jesus' teaching in every area urges us to live in a way which reflects the love God has for us, and is radically obedient to the will of God.

Divorce is as negative a thing as it is possible to imagine; it involves the destruction of hopes and the loss of love. But the experience of divorce should not be seen simply as a negative thing. It will be hard to explain what I mean by this, because it involves an association of divorce with sinfulness—though not necessarily with personal sin—on the one hand, and on the other it involves an experience so painful that it is hard to see anything redeeming about it at all.

Divorce does involve failure. It isn't simply a matter of two people "not being right for one another;" that sort of language is too simple-minded to deserve analysis. It means one or both parties giving up on something that matters deeply. It means the death in one or two people of the attention and respect which are the heart of love. It means that one partner in marriage, or both partners, form an image of the other which is limited, small, somehow diminished, and believe it to be true. Divorce is a dead end. And in some cases it should happen. I know of marriages which went on for years with both parents hating one another, at terrible cost to their children. I know of a marriage in which the husband was so constantly demanding, rude, boorish, and selfish that when the marriage ended everyone who knew the couple felt relieved; and in another marriage the woman was so thoroughly domineering that those around her could have no life of their own. But marriages of this extreme sort, as well as marriages which end on more confusing grounds, involve sin at its most basic level.

It is usual to take a moralistic view of sin: we see it as a personal failure, a lapse in willing, a temporary collapse of the presence of mind which we would like to believe is our ordinary waking state. But sin is a more profound and radical thing than that; it isn't simply a personal failure, but a condition, a climate, It is something we can find ourselves in, without much apparent help. It is a sign of our helplessness and need for God.

It is possible for people to find themselves in a situation which in every way seems not to be of their making, certainly not of their present willing, not something they would will if a contrary willing could change it; and at the same time it is the result of decisions they made, without full awareness of the consequences of those decisions; in that sense it is something they can be said to be responsible for. And it is a situation which is in every apparent way destructive and painful, and there is no good way out. Marriages can end up this way. It would be good if they did not; it would be good if we could make reconciliation happen..It would be good if we lived in a world where we were all bottomless fountains of forgiveness and compassion, and divinity could have its way with us.

But the world is at least as sad as it seems to be sometimes. And people who did not intend things to happen the way they happen often end up suffering, feeling in their bones that their suffering is unfair and undeserved because it came without warning; it was in no way the consequence of the ordinary rational thing we think of as good behavior. At the same time people caught this way can feel tremendous guilt, seeing the connections between their decisions and their present state.

Our ordinary sense of sin is too self-conscious, and doesn't pay enough attention to this more radical darkness, the understanding of the world as a fallen place where sin is a condition more than a deed. But this sense of sin is necessary before we can know our radical need for God. Those who accept it fully, accepting forgiveness with it, are much closer to the truth than people who are virtuous in the legalistic sense of the word, but have no understanding of the darkness which surrounds them. The strength which can be found in weakness is a living truth for many men and women; some of them have learned from the experience of divorce, others from encounters with their own weakness where alcohol or drugs are concerned. (The latter example is in some ways less complicated than that of divorce. The responsibility for addiction finally lies with the addict, and that understanding is liberating. But the responsibility for divorce is rarely a clear thing; it is in learning to live with that lack of clarity that the divorced person can begin to experience forgiveness and personal reconciliation.)

What about those who marry again after divorce? The current canon laws don't permit this for Catholics. Unless a person gets an annul-

ment—unless he or she is able to argue successfully
that no marriage existed in the first place—remarriage is forbidden, and those who do remarry are not
admitted to communion.

This has not always been the case in Catholic
history, and the changing attitudes of many priests
and laypeople suggest that it may not be the case in
the future. I believe that it is more honest to admit
that a marriage can exist, and can fail. What I would
like to see is hardly the point, but for what it is worth
(and I realize that this will not satisfy a good many
people on both sides of the question) I would like to
see the church continue to refuse a Catholic wedding to people whose original marriage partners are
still alive; and I would also like to see people who
have remarried, believing it to be the only possible
choice for them, admitted to communion. This
seems to me better than the current, somewhat
hypocritical annulment procedure, and it would
underscore the Catholic emphasis on the permanence of marriage. At the same time, it would not
remove Catholics who have remarried after divorce
from the vital center of their faith, the eucharist.
Christ's presence in the eucharist was never meant
as a reward for good behavior, and his call to do this
in remembrance of him was not qualified.

HOMOSEXUALITY

THIS subject is one which no one can be objective about, and nobody's generalizations are terribly impressive. For years the mainstream of moral theory said that homosexuality was morally wrong, a sinful thing if indulged, a disorder; more recently it was called a sickness, something wrong with a person who might be all right in every other area of his life. This has been challenged during the past several years by those who argue that homosexuality, although statistically abnormal (like being a redhead is, or being lefthanded), is not necessarily a sickness or a moral fault. It is not enough to point at years of tradition to justify our attitude on this subject. There are few theologians today who would accept the attitudes of John Chrysostom or Martin Luther towards Jews, or Thomas Aquinas' attitude towards women. Many patristic and later pronouncements on the subject of women are based on pre-Christian attitudes. Simply because it has ancient warrant we do not believe that women are unclean or tainted because of the blood curse of their menstrual cycles.

What if our attitude towards homosexuality were the same sort of problem? It is true that there are those whose attitude towards women calls into question our alleged advances in the area of women's rights, but for the most part we seem to have realized that the previous taboos involving women, and the notion that they were inferior to men, were wrong. What if we are similarly wrong about homosexuality? It is important not to assume without examination that the traditional attitude towards homosexuality is correct, because matters of charity and justice are at stake.

Those looking for final answers to the question will not find them here; that is beyond the scope of this chapter, and also beyond my capability. But I do want to raise some questions which ought to guide an inquiry into the subject.

The strongest argument against homosexuality has been that it is "unnatural." We are, after all, made in two sexes; we are, most of us, naturally attracted to the opposite sex, and this attraction has not only produced a large measure of delight for the individuals involved, but has secured the survival of the human race.

As a practicing heterosexual I can understand the appeal of this argument, but it is not without its problems. First of all, mere naturalness is not always the best defense for any form of behavior. It is natural to attack those who surprise you, to yell out in frustration when opposed in any way, to kill your enemy, preferably when his back is turned, and to defecate whenever the urge is felt. However, it is not civilized or moral to do these things. To a large extent, civilization is a series of victories over mere naturalness; and heterosexual naturalness includes the hideously common crime of rape. Here we are speaking of naturalness as the unfettered expression of appetites and passion, however. Homosexuality doesn't seem to fall quite into that category. But what about the fact that animals prefer the opposite sex?

Two things are wrong here. One is that animals don't, always; the other is that animal preferences are not offered to us as guides to proper human behavior in other areas. There are animals who indulge in homosexual behavior, even when not deprived of normal heterosexual possibilities. Homosexuality has also occurred in too many human societies to see it simply as a perverse taste learned by pathetic people from depraved English schoolmasters. It has been dealt with tolerantly and intolerantly at different times and in different cultures. John Boswell's *Christianity, Social Tolerance, and Homosexuality* claims (with impressive historical evidence) that although it was not quite sanctioned it was tolerated during much of the medieval period in the Christian West, much more so than it has been in recent centuries. Some commentators have tried to show that societies in which homosexuality was tolerated were ones in which women were held in low esteem (for example, certain segments of Islamic society and periods in ancient Greek history); but this doesn't hold up, because there were societies in which women were considered chattel which were also strongly condemnatory where homosexuality was concerned. There have been other attempts to tie tolerance of homosexuality to high birthrates, and intolerance to a need for more births. But the fact is that no clear link has been made between the status of women or demographic pressures and the tolerance of homosexuality, nothing, anyway, so strong as to be persuasive to someone determined to take a stand on the other side, whatever it may be.

The mainstream of Catholic moral theology has held that homosexual acts are sinful, but the mere fact of being a homosexual is morally neutral. Homosexual acts are unnatural because they cannot lead to new life. The same argument has been used by many moral theologians against any sexual act which involves contraception or withdrawal—any sexual act which is not formally open to conception (even if that might be impossible owing to the time of month or natural sterility) is seen as unnatural and therefore sinful. One theologian reversed his qualified acceptance of contraception on the grounds that the arguments which made it acceptable could also be seen as applying to homosexuality.

The Catholic theological consensus, however, differs from the fundamentalist in that it does not see homosexuality itself as a sinful thing, or as something which is necessarily a result of sin, unless this includes the whole wide range of those unfortunate things which come under the heading of the Fall and the damage it has done to just about everything, in which case homosexuality joins every other human predilection, from the appetite for real estate and money to many heterosexual desires, or the selfish uses of solitude.

There are some recent opinions and conjectures, based on establishable facts, which raise some doubts about the traditional consensus. While it is a mistake to assume that every recent opinion is in and of itself superior to a more traditional understanding, it is also a mistake to dismiss recent opinions simply on the grounds that they are recent and conflict with tradition (as if tradition itself began nowhere but was always around, being permanent and unchangeable). It simply doesn't work to ignore the evidences of anthropology and psychology which suggest, however awkward this might be for those who think of homosexuality as a perverse choice, that homosexuality is a human constant and has very little to do with choice. If practical morality concerns itself primarily with choice, as it necessarily must, then homosexuality is not primarily a matter which concerns practical morality. The question for the homosexual is not "should I be homosexual?" so much as it is "given the fact that I am who I am, what should I do?" And this is, of course, the same question which faces the heterosexual, who also did not choose his less difficult place in the world but, like the homosexual, finds himself there, in the middle of everything, with some important questions. So far there is nothing which would contradict Catholic tradition, but there are some questions raised by the fact that homosexuality is not a matter of choice, and they have not been handled particularly well.

The fact is that Christianity has traditionally placed marriage at the center of its approach to Christian sexuality. I believe that this placing is right, and cannot understand marriage apart from the possibility of children—that is to say, it seems to me that sexuality is at its richest and deepest when it can lead to new life. It is true that "new life" can be a metaphor, and the renewal which sex in a loving context can bring can certainly exist apart from reproduction; but there is a fullness about the sex which can lead to another life which is uniquely wonderful, and worthy of special celebration. This is a central aspect of our celebration of matrimony, and it is properly at the center of our approach to sex—a sun around which other planets move. There are some things so common that we can be blinded to how wonderful they are. The fact that people can be moved out of love to make love to one another, and that from their lovemaking another life can begin, is one of them.

What I have to say here is absolutely personal, and will not satisfy anyone who takes a clear either/or position on the subject of homosexuality. I have friends who are homosexual and friends who are heterosexual (I hope this doesn't put me into the "some of my best friends" category); I have more of the latter than of the former, which is statistically predictable. All that I can say about this subject with any assurance is that one group seems as decent as the other. A couple of the homosexuals are professed Christians, active in their churches, and they are deeply hurt by the attitudes which they encounter from their fellow churchfolk. They have felt the need to conceal their homosexuality from people they like very much. Those who have felt that they should not conceal it have paid a price for making it public, even in a careful way. There is something profoundly unfair about this.

The assumptions of heterosexuals about homosexuality is too often an unexamined belief that we (us hets) are healthy, and they (the homos) are not. The odd range of sexual behavior is not seen in its variety but is confined—for this purpose—to a strictly moral plane, a plane in which right and wrong are seen as everything; but even this is overcoated with a false clinical layer in which sickness and health are used as code words which really mean badness and goodness.

But sexual morality has been reduced to something mechanistic when sex is understood as good or morally acceptable because it happens between members of the opposite sex, and wrong when it happens between members of the same sex. I am afraid that the average Christian would accept the notion that a heterosexual Don Juan is in some essential way healthier than a homosexual who is faithful to one person.

There is an ideal sense in which sexual intercourse happens at its fullest and richest between married men and women who are fully aware of their symbolic importance as representatives of the relationship between Christ and the church; and there is the fact that most of the times married people make love this is not at all the case; and perhaps always trying to be ideal is not even a desireable thing—it may keep you from learning the lessons of the moment, lessons which cannot be learned when you are "trying to be" anything at all. The sacrament married people participate in, in their love-making and in other ways, is something they learn and grow into as they go along. Many married people would agree that, whatever reality they may experience sacramentally, it was not at all clear to them during the early years of their marriage. The meaning of a sacrament reveals itself slowly; it is elicited between a man and a woman by the symbol of marriage, which embodies the fullness which may eventually be manifested in the reality of a particular marriage. The love which grows in marriage takes time, care, and attention; it doesn't just happen to us, and at the same time it is not simply something we will, or make to happen all by ourselves. It happens because of our attention and willing, but our attention and willing do not create it or cause it. They give love an occasion to make itself present. All real love is a gift of God.

What does this have to do with homosexuality? This, I think: for the Christian homosexual, just as for the Christian heterosexual, promiscuity is ruled out: it trivializes and fatally limits what sex is meant to be. But an argument can be made for the case that, if we can admit the morality of sex which cannot be reproductive (for example, sex between people too old to conceive, or a couple one of whom is sterile, not to speak of contraceptive sex) it is necessary at least to consider the possibility that a faithful homosexual relationship is not by definition an immoral thing.

The current mainstream Catholic opinion is that homosexuals should be celibate. This may indeed be the safest way, morally, but safety and the need for it have not always called forth the best things, morally or otherwise, in people. On the other hand, the argument that because celibacy is extremely difficult for many people is not, in and of itself, an impressive reason for rejecting it. Difficulty is part of the Christian life. Celibacy or chastity may at times be an apparent rejection of what seems to be a blessing. A celibate priest or nun, or a married man or woman, may fall in love with someone, and remain chaste or celibate for the sake of something higher. However, it isn't at all clear to many Christian homosexuals that they are remaining celibate for the sake of something higher. They are asked to remain celibate (and celibacy has, in the case of the priesthood, been advanced as a gift to the church, a charism like prophecy) primarily to avoid sin; and they are not sure that their sexual orientation is one which necessarily leads to sin.

The pastoral approach of many confessors and other spiritual directors is, increasingly, to say that where celibacy does not seem to be right or possible, fidelity is essential, and to make it clear that promiscuity is inconsistent with the gospel. The rest is left to God's love.

The Christian homosexual has a rough time of it. It is easy for people who have never experienced any homosexual feelings to find something so strange in the subject that an acute discomfort prevents them from seeing it compassionately. My own feeling is mixed: homosexuality may indeed be a neurosis, a case of arrested development; but this argument has been made by heterosexuals who can hardly be said to be disinterested, and if it is only a neurosis, the reaction against it has been at least as neurotic, and truly ugly. Homosexuality may, on the other hand, be the sexual equivalent of left-handedness.

I really don't know. I am not willing to trust what may be merely an ancient prejudice, like the blood-prejudice against menstruating women; its ancientness does not make it a form of wisdom. I am not prepared to look at historical prejudice as a final guide to the question. Nor am I willing to trust the latest psychiatric opinion to come down the pike. The point is that my attitudes towards people can serve as barriers. Paul says that he not only does not judge others; he does not even judge himself. What in all cases I cannot deny is that any self-sacrificing, self-giving love is holy, and the love between two people is holy. It may be that a faithful homosexual relationship participates in some way in the sacramental reality which marriage is meant to reflect. Certainly, if love is there, something divine is there with it.